Love, Peace, and Wisdom in Education

in Education

A Vision for Education in the 21st Century

Jing Lin

ROWMAN & LITTLEFIELD EDUCATION
Lanham, Maryland • Toronto • Oxford
2006

Published in the United States of America
by Rowman & Littlefield Education
A Division of Rowman & Littlefield Publishers, Inc.
A wholly owned subsidary of The Rowman & Littlefield Publishing Group, Inc.
4501 Forbes Boulevard, Suite 200, Lanham, Maryland 20706
www.rowmaneducation.com

PO Box 317
Oxford
OX2 9RU, UK

British Library Cataloguing in Publication Information Available

Library of Congress Cataloging-in-Publication Data

Lin, Jing, 1962-
  Love, peace, and wisdom in education : a vision for education in the
21st century / Jing Lin.
      p. cm.
  Includes bibliographical references.
  ISBN-13: 978-1-57886-334-1 (hardcover : alk. paper)
  ISBN-13: 978-1-57886-333-4 (pbk. : alk. paper)
  ISBN-10: 1-57886-334-1 (hardcover : alk. paper)
  ISBN-10: 1-57886-333-3 (pbk. : alk. paper)
  1. Education—Aims and objectives. 2. Social change. 3. Love. 4. Peace.
5. Wisdom. I. Title.
  LB14.7.L556 2006
  370'.1—dc22
                                                      2005023110

∞™ The paper used in this publication meets the minimum requirements of
American National Standard for Information Sciences—Permanence of
Paper for Printed Library Materials, ANSI/NISO Z39.48-1992.
Manufactured in the United States of America.

This book is dedicated to Dr. Yan Xin,
my teacher of life.

Contents

Acknowledgments

This is a book that one has to write with one's life. For a book on orienting education for love must come from a life experience of understanding life, living with love, and working for love.

I have learned unconditional love from my parents and grandmother. I have been given the example of a father who gives unconditionally and has been unselfish and integral his entire life; I have been influenced by a grandmother who was illiterate but knew what it took to live a life with no regrets; and I benefit from a mother who takes life in perspective and always maintains calmness and openness.

I have learned love from my teachers, colleagues, friends, students, and strangers. Looking back on my path, my life has been sustained by the work of others, out of love.

I came to know that there is an all-encompassing love in the universe only after I met Dr. Yan Xin and began to cultivate an authentic, traditional Chinese qi energy cultivation system. Opening myself to all life forces and the energies in the universe, I experience the interconnectedness of all people and all existences. My most astounding experience came one day when, after visiting the Great Wall, I literally heard the pounding of a great heart in the universe. This heart was pumping into all existences a love so profound that it is utterly beyond description. The whole universe pulsates with this love. I was completely awestruck and moved beyond words. As the love penetrated my cells, I was transformed and realized we need to reveal this essence to others. I realized that we have solutions to all of our major problems if we choose to love each other as our beloved brothers and sisters—rather than hate each other—and if we care for nature like we care for ourselves. Since that day, all people I meet, regardless of their race, gender, and cultural background, appear to me like my own family members.

Since knowing this great love, I have learned that love is joy, love is our life's purpose, and love is our calling. Opening my spiritual eyes to see the loving energy in the universe, I realized our fundamental oneness. We are one, and we are inextricably bound by love.

It is based on this profound transformation that I started to explore solutions to our world's gravest challenges. I see that despite wars raging in our world, the power of love can help us transcend hatred and eventually prevail. I see the need to change our attitude toward nature and learn to coexist with other species as a global ecofamily. This book is an outflow of my realization and understandings from this incredible experience. For this, my deepest gratitude goes to Dr. Yan Xin, who opens up my energy system to flow in synchronicity with the love of the universe.

Seeking to know more about our world, I have traveled among our world's teachings about life. I have been deeply influenced by Eastern philosophy and world philosophy in the large. I embrace the teaching of virtues and love in all religions and philosophies and receive my inspiration from studying many cultures and religions in the world. For this, I wish to thank ancient and modern sages and people around the world who share their wisdom and vision.

I would also like to thank my family: my parents-in-law, who have given me their loving kindness throughout the past ten years without any hesitation; my husband, who is my friend, teacher, and cheerleader; and, finally, my lovely children, Eirene and Erica, who teach me the power of unconditional love and help me to know that children are our students as well as our teachers.

Introduction

> We have been forced to a point where we're going to have to grapple with the problems that men have been trying to grapple with through history, but the demands didn't force them to do it. Survival demands that we grapple with them. Men, for years now, have been talking about war and peace. But now, no longer can they just talk about it. It is no longer a choice between violence and nonviolence in this world; it's nonviolence or nonexistence. (Martin Luther King Jr., "I See the Promised Land," April 3, 1968)

We are living in an age of rapid scientific and technological innovation. The advancement of information technology in the past three decades has broken down the limitation of geographical distance, making communication among people around the world instantaneous; the completion of the DNA blueprint has opened up a new chapter in human life and medical research, leading us to ponder, more than ever, the questions, What is life? What do we know and what do we not know? However, we are also living in an age of major crises. In the 20th century, two world wars broke out that resulted in the loss of 150 million lives as "more people died in the wars of the 20th century than at any other time in history" (Smith and Carson 1998, p. ix). Into the beginning of the twenty-first century, military might is believed to be a deterrent for war and a guarantee of safety, and countries are competing to build more powerful and lethal weapons of mass destruction. We now possess nuclear bombs and weapons that can kill the human species and destroy the Earth many times over. Since the tragedy of September 11, 2001, global conflicts have intensified, and more than ever tensions are felt among people from different cultures and beliefs. As concerned global citizens, we are reminded daily of the urgency for all global citizens to take comprehensive actions to promote international peace and understanding in all aspects of our life.

Environmentally, we face the devastation of polluted rivers and air, global warming and greenhouse effects, ozone depletion, and extinction of animal and plant species (Milburn 2000). We pay a heavy price for a development paradigm that centers on human beings' greed and relentless exploitation of our Mother Nature, seeing her as passive objects to be controlled and manipulated. Consumerism and materialism have taken over our lives, leading many people to believe that life is just an endless process of seeking more wealth and greater power. Success is defined in monetary terms or in terms of power and status, rather than as service and selfless giving.

Scientific, positivistic paradigms in the last hundred years have dominated our thinking. When we adopt a reductionist worldview, the human body, mind, and spirit are split into separate entities. While a tremendous amount of energy was put into scientific discoveries about what happens "out there," the scientific community has done very little to understand humans as whole beings who are rational as well as emotional, moral, spiritual, and ecological. In our attempt to be "objective and neutral," we marginalize moral and ethical values, taking them out of the public sphere and our education system at our own peril. We have shunned the discussion of spirituality in the public arena (Myers 2000), attaching many taboos to the teaching of spirituality.

In education today, young people are experiencing profound spiritual and emotional crises. Teachers are uncertain about what they need to teach, and students are increasingly feeling a huge void in their lives, not knowing where they are going. Many are addicted to drugs.

To a great extent, many of the problems we are experiencing result from our failure to recognize ourselves as holistic, interconnected beings who need to cultivate our abilities to embrace the world with unconditional love and care. Our lives have been organized on the assumption of separation: a separation of ourselves from each other, a separation of our destiny with our environment, and a separation of our bodies and minds from our hearts and spirit. The debate on school reform, which began during the mid-1980s, has focused on the imposition of external standards on teachers and has neglected the issues that concern the core issue of who we are and what we want to become, as individuals and as a human race, especially in the current context of global conflicts and environmental and social crises.

In face of the realities we are living in, a paradigm shift in education is urgently called for. We need education that facilitates the formation of a compassionate and loving global community, and one that teaches the younger generation to form a harmonious, respectful relationship with nature. Goals of education need to be shifted from a rationalistic, functionalist perspective that primarily emphasizes tests and efficiency, to a constructive, transformative paradigm that stresses love-based, care-based education that helps nurture understanding and respect for all human beings and nature. We should educate the new generation in a way that adds meaning and purpose to their daily lives by helping them learn to forgive, respect, and appreciate others, to harbor great compassion and unconditional love for all human beings and all existences. Throughout this process, long-held beliefs and practices in education must be critically examined. In all, constructing a loving world should be the central purpose of education in the 21st century.

Education in the 20th century has left us with many major problems that are beginning to have a serious impact. We have trained people to use their minds sharply but have largely neglected to cultivate their hearts and souls with love and compassion. Students spend a good part of their life in schools that are becoming spiritual wastelands—students come out of school without having formed a strong sense of purpose in life, developed virtuous characters, or cultivated a sense of responsibility for the construction of a loving and peaceful world. Consequently, we have turned out citizens who feel neither remorse nor any sense of guilt while killing innocent people or using their highly trained brains to build the most lethal weapons to kill the largest number of people possible. Furthermore, we have trained loyal citizens who surrender their power to leaders who spend billions of dollars on building weapons of mass destruction, while educators, parents, and children are crying for funding for quality education, and millions of people have no health care or are living in debilitating poverty. Compared with military expenditure, we spend a paltry amount on programs that provide opportunities for people around the world to make contact with each other and to build international and cross-cultural understanding and respect at an intimate level. We limit the vision of our young people to using education mainly to find a well-paid job, failing to enlighten them to see that our life is a precious gift with which we can expand our ability to love and care, to bring light to this world and kindle hope in others. We strive to meet external criteria for success and neglect reflection and inner transformation. Policy-makers and scholars call for teachers to implement numerous initiatives, but seldom are teachers given a voice to discuss what they believe in their hearts is important for the children. We turn out citizens who are savvy about violence on TV and in video games, and who look dispassionately at killings in wars and conflicts raging in the world because of years of desensitization. As a society, we allow the media and entertainment industry to make a huge profit on selling killing! We do little to prevent our younger generation from becoming wasteful and frivolous people while starvation is raging in many parts of the world.

School for love in the 21st century is a form of education this book endeavors to envision and develop. It is a school committed to the construction of a loving society, to usher in long-lasting global peace and ecological survival. It is a school that realizes the great potentials of all students—the capacity to love and care, to transcend anger and hatred, to imagine a new world, and to work constructively and cooperatively for the building of a beloved global community as envisioned by Martin Luther King.

What is love? Dr. King puts it very eloquently:

> I have discovered that the highest good is love. This principle is at the center of the cosmos. It is the great unifying force of life. (King 1963a, p. 133).
>
> When I speak of love, I am speaking of that force which all the great religions have seen as the supreme unifying principle of life. Love is the key that unlocks the door which leads to the ultimate reality. (King, 1967a)

Similarly, Gandhi says the following:

> Scientists tell us that without the presence of the cohesive force amongst atoms that comprise the globe of ours, it would crumble to pieces and we would cease to exist; and as there is a cohesive force in blind matter, so must there be in all things animate, and the name for that cohesive force among animate beings is love.
>
> True love is boundless like the ocean and, swelling within one, spreads itself out and, crossing all boundaries and frontiers, envelops the whole world.
>
> It is my firm belief that it is love that sustains the earth. There only is life where there is love.
>
> The law of love, call it attraction, affinity, cohesion if you like, governs the world. (Gandhi 1999, pp. 55–57)

Drawing from King's and Gandhi's wisdom, and based on my own experience and understanding, the love I am referring to in this book is the creative, primordial energy that flows in the collective unconscious of all people and all that exists in the universe. It is the energy, matter, eco/spiritual/informational essence all combined that creates cohesion and awareness of interconnectedness, and brings a common purpose to all existence. Love is the energy that warms the heart and lights up the soul. It is what makes it possible for human beings and all other existences to build, nurture, bond, and experience the joys that flow from tapping into the wisdom of the soul and spirit.

It is this love that makes us want to be good, that implants a conscience in us so we know what is right or wrong in all circumstances, even though we may deny it. This love connects all of us on Earth as brothers and sisters. As the Chinese sage Mo Zi says, this "interconnected Love" causes us to see all people in the world as our own body, our superior as ourselves, our subordinate as ourselves, others' houses as our own house, others' country as our own country. Mo Zi concludes that with this love, countries will not fight each other, families will not have upheaval, stealing will stop, government will function in harmony, and the whole world will have peace. "If people in the world all love like this, we have peace; if we go against this, we have chaos. This is why we *must* convince others to love each other." (Wang Bin 2001, p. 62)

In this book, a school in the 21st century is envisioned to be a school for love. The school for love is built on the belief that human beings are inextricably linked by the energy of love, which gives life to all people and all existences in the universe. Love is the energy, information, matter, and spirit that interlink the spirits and souls of all existences. As human beings, we are by nature kind and loving. We are part of the universe's loving energy. As love is the energy that creates the universe, love is also the energy that sustains human existence. The fact that we fall into incessant conflicts and hatred is due to a lack of understanding of this essence in ourselves.

In this book, education for peace is perceived to be a top priority in future schools. Peace entails not only disarmament; it also pertains to the construction of a culture of love and respect. Peace is sustained not only by international and national organizations, but more importantly by global citizens who have hearts full of compassion and love for each other.

In the 21st century, we are shifting from a material civilization that operates on the laws of the jungle to a spiritual civilization in which our expanded awareness of the self and the universe leads to an identification of all people and all existences as an interconnected family. Our loving community includes not only human beings but also all species, animate or inanimate, sentient or insentient, in the ecological cosmos. The new education I envision focuses on cultivating our heart's capacity to care for and love others as we do ourselves, which is based on a deep understanding that *loving others pertains to loving ourselves*. This process is reciprocal and energizing. Such a realization will enlighten us toward a world for love, and a world for all.

This book invites educators, teachers, researchers, leaders, and students, in fact all those who are concerned with our well-being, to dialogue about and ponder what we should do to herald a new paradigm in education in the 21st century. This paradigm is about building a new world through the power of love. Treading on this path, we may not have a lot of supporters at the beginning, but taking the first steps is crucial. With courage, we will overcome all obstacles in the way of the gigantic task of building a new world through schools for love, family for love, community for love, society for love, and world for love. Love is the hope of the 21st century.

This book is composed of nine chapters. The following is a brief outline of each chapter.

Chapter 1 discusses the deep crises facing the human race, such as global violence, environmental destruction, and moral and spiritual breakdown in society. It examines the critical importance for the human race to act *now* to address how we can educate our younger generation to live as a global family, to be in harmony with nature, and to have a sound understanding about life's meaning and purpose. The chapter criticizes current paradigms in science and social science that emphasize relentless exploitation of the Earth's resources, ruthless competition for power and profit, and disengagement of our body, mind, and spirit in the pursuit of "objective truth." It criticizes the anthropocentric view in social development theories that posit human beings as the center of the universe, who have the right to subject all species on Earth for human greed. The chapter examines how nihilism is destroying our sense of purpose in life, and how destructive competitiveness, social injustice, and inequalities are breaking our bonds as equal fellow human beings. The chapter suggests that piecemeal reform in education can do very little to transform our society and ensure our collective survival, hence a new paradigm must be envisioned and brought to life.

Chapter 2 postulates a new philosophy and a new epistemology based on the centrality of love. The main point is that by nature we are essentially loving beings. I cite current scientific research and writings to support the argument that love is a positive energy that nurtures the body, mind, and spirit. I review scientific experiments that show that expressing good wishes in one's heart (such as through prayer) can help patients significantly improve their health. I argue that not only human beings thrive on love, even plants and animals need it as nutrition. I argue that human life, and in fact all existences in the universe, is created for the purpose of sharing and experiencing love. Love is a powerful force that enables life to continue. Only love can subdue hatred, as has been argued powerfully by Mahatma Gandhi and Martin Luther King Jr., among others.

I also examine developments in quantum physics that indicate we are living in an interconnected world, and our emotions and feelings have everything to do with the well-being of ourselves and those people and things in the environment. The chapter also discusses Eastern philosophy, especially Chinese philosophy and its practice in Chinese medicine, which holds that yin and yang energy propelled by love creates all forms of life and regulates the relationship of nature, humanity, and the universe (for example, the sun gives yang energy, and the moon gives yin energy). In Taoism and Buddhism (Conze 2001), unconditional love for all beings and existences is essential for one to attain the highest level of spiritual development. Love is the primordial energy that connects and sustains all creations.

This chapter serves the purpose to deconstruct the notion of otherness, of separation of our being with our environment.

Chapter 3 argues that 21st-century education needs to undergo a dramatic shift from schools based on an efficiency model to that of school for love. The chapter outlines ways in which school goals, curriculum, and teacher-student relationships are reorganized to make learning to love and care the central theme of education. The chapter argues that schooling should start with affirming children's good nature. I propose a new pedagogy, which sees school as the site that teaches love, care, and respect for our family, community, the global world, and all existences in the universe. Educators should empower students with propensities and skills to care and make connections. They are role models of unconditional love and compassion.

The chapter suggests ways schools for love can provide students with the daily experience of working cooperatively, the joy of giving and receiving love, forgiving and understanding each other, bridging gaps, and building bonds. The goal of school for love is to help students form strong values and habits as loving people.

For children to become loving beings, schools need to pay attention to human qualities that have long been ignored. Chapter 4 calls for the integrated development of IQ, EQ (emotional intelligence), MQ (moral intelligence), SQ (spiritual intelligence), and Eco-Q (ecological intelligence). The chapter defines EQ as the ability to connect with each other and bring balance and harmony to life; MQ is defined as the ability to share love and care, to have compassion, and to forgive and respect. SQ is defined as the ability to look deep into ourselves and understand intuitively and spiritually who we are, in connection with the spirit of all people and creations in the universe. It is also to act responsibly and make wise judgments in daily life and at times of crisis. Eco-Q is wisdom regarding human relationship with nature, and attributes and abilities we use to protect and preserve our environment. The chapter suggests that schools for love should aim at cultivating wisdom rather than placing a simple-minded emphasis on students' intellectual development.

The chapter argues that only with the integrated development of IQ, EQ, MQ, SQ, and Eco-Q do we turn a person into an educated being. This chapter challenges educators to expand their teaching methods, to incorporate those that help students to explore their inner hearts and deeper selves. The chapter discusses the "soft" areas that have been ignored in education and reviews traditional and modern teaching methods that enable students to cultivate their emotional, moral, and spiritual growth. Eastern philosophy holds that a person is essentially a moral being. All the world's great religions contain practices that nurture the heart and soul. The chapter challenges educators to go into these new frontiers with courage, to explore more effective ways to transform future global citizens from the inside. The chapter stresses that such integrated development necessarily requires a change of teacher-student relationship, characterized by emotional and spiritual connection, trust, and mutual exploration of the meaning of life. In such a relationship, the top-down hierarchy is broken by an understanding that children have as much to teach adults as adults have to teach them. Students are empowered to see that life's purpose is not only to live a better material life but also to have a wise and meaningful spiritual life.

Chapter 5 argues that in the 21st century, priority must be given to education for global peace. There is a great need to educate children to learn lessons from the horrible mistakes we have made. The chapter discusses different dimensions of peace education. Teachers are seen as peace educators who integrate peace education into all aspects of their teaching. I also discuss the relationship between peace and virtues, peace and intelligence.

Chapter 6 focuses on the love for nature, for the universe, for all life forms and all existences. Humans are perceived as custodians other than dominators of nature. "Feminine qualities" that stress care and service are elevated to their cosmic importance, to emphasize the need for a balanced world of femininity and masculinity, for mutual interdependence and interconnectedness. This understanding applies to the relationship between humankind and all existences on Earth and in the universe. Development of a holistic, interconnected perspective in our relationship with nature is another priority of education in the 21st century.

Chapter 7 discusses the shortfalls in current debates on school reform. The chapter highlights the nearsightedness of school reform discussions and outlines issues that are central to the building of a better world through education. Education is not effective without the cultivation of wisdom. Realignment of our debate on current issues in education so that we see the dire need for rekindling the desire among professionals and students for the pursuit of wisdom is fundamental.

Chapter 8 looks into the role leaders must take to build a world based on love. The chapter calls for a deeply reconstituted notion of leadership, vitally different from the current paradigm of authority and domination. The new leadership is discussed through the lens of service, love, and care. The need for vision and courage is also discussed.

Finally, Chapter 9 argues that if schools for love are to enable students to become persons who care deeply, who integrate compassion and love into every facet of their lives, families and communities must be engaged, and their influence should vibrate out to the larger society and the world, in a global effort for human collective transformation based on the power of love.

In the 20th century, important books charted the course of educational development, such as *Experience and Education* by John Dewey, *Deschooling Society* by Ivan Illich, and *Pedagogy of the Oppressed* by Paulo Freire, all of which call for dramatic shifts in education. *A Nation at Risk*, a U.S. Department of Education document issued in 1985, shifted national attention to accountability and standardization in education. I believe that none of these books and documents lift us up to the height of seeing the need for assuring the fundamental survival of humanity through education for love.

This book by no means negates efforts made by educators and thinkers who have made great attempts to transform our world. Rather, with it I hope to form only a small wave of a big trend toward returning to the "basics" of who we are and what we should become. Many books have recently come out that emphasize the role of education in teaching love and care, in awakening our spirit and the need for holistic education. I see this book as an endeavor to join this effort.

Chapter One

Paradigm Shifts in Human Consciousness

As a human race, we are facing challenges of huge proportions, including global wars and violence. Moreover, the possibility of devastating breakdown in our environment is looming large, as witnessed in the South Asian tsunami in December 2004 that killed nearly a quarter million people. As a human race, we have built weapons of mass destruction—nuclear and biological—that are able to wipe everyone from the face of the planet many times over! However, as the Chinese word "crisis" denotes, opportunities are embedded in crises. The possibility of annihilating ourselves has brought to the fore the awareness that we must embrace a global ethic of universal love and unconditional forgiveness and reconciliation to have a future. More and more people are convinced that the power of love is more profound than any weapon or war machine. Environmental devastation and the resulting disasters have awakened more people than ever to the awareness of our collective identity as a global family and residents of Mother Earth. Our decisions determine our future—with love we survive and prosper; with hatred we cannot have peace or survive.

This chapter discusses the deep crises facing the human race, such as global violence, environmental destruction, and moral and spiritual breakdown in society. These crises call for a shift in our thinking and priorities. Education is the hope of humanity's future because school is a place where we can reshape the heart and soul of our future global citizens. In the search for solutions to the problems in our world, we need to construct our education to be a school for love and profoundly transform our world with this new paradigm.

CRISES FACING THE HUMAN RACE TODAY

Global Violence—Wars, Conflicts, Crimes

We are living in an environment that is more violent than ever. Every day in the world there is bloodshed caused by regional conflicts, internal wars, murders, political persecutions, ideological or religious differences, social injustices and inequalities, and so forth. A huge arsenal of weapons of massive destruction, capable of completely annihilating the human race and wiping out all life on earth, creates a huge shadow over our future. More and more the world is tilted toward imbalance—imbalance between the voice of peace and violence, between hatred and forgiveness. Wars are waged in the name of religion, of national security and interests, of ideological convictions, and of tribal and personal vengeance. Hatred and bigotry are legitimized under the rhetoric of righteousness, openly or silently approved by a large number of people, many of whom are highly educated. Prejudices and stereotypes have perpetuated cultural disrespect and reinforced misunderstanding among people.

Environmental Destruction and Devastation

> In the 24 hours since this time yesterday, over 200,000 acres of rain-forest have been destroyed in our world. Fully 13 million tons of toxic chemicals have been released into our environment. Over 45,000 people have died of starvation, 38,000 of them children. And more than 130 plant or animal species have been driven to extinction by the actions of humans. (The last time there was such a rapid loss of species was when the dinosaurs vanished.) And all this just since yesterday. (Hartmann 1999, p. 1)

This quote by Hartmann illustrates well the rapidity and seriousness of environmental destruction. With industrial revolution, scientific discoveries, and technological innovations, our world is materially wealthier than at any period in human history; however, never in history have human beings been more destructive toward the natural environment than today. Taking external criteria such as wealth and power to define our value and success, human beings have engaged in an endless struggle for the control of natural resources with little concern for the well-being of future generations. The business world's visions for the future are restricted by short-term concern for profits, and governments yield to pressure from powerful special interest groups and shortchange principles to accommodate their interests. In the global pursuit of a life style that is frivolous and unsustainable, we suffer the consequences of polluted rivers, rapidly shrinking forests, desertification, the extinction of animals and plants, the drying up of oil and gas that have accumulated over billions of years. . . . Global warming, ozone layer depletion, natural disasters, strange weather—are all signs that warn us about the dire consequence of our behaviors. Unfortunately, many governments and a large number of people in the world are not heeding these signs.

Globalization escalates the competition for profits, drastically accelerating the depletion of resources, with "strong" countries making all attempts to control resources and grab from the "weaker" countries. Weapons of mass destruction are traded among countries as a "normal" form of economic activity, and countries spend billions of dollars building weapons of insane destructive power in the name of protecting "national interests" or to ensure that the "just" force can win over "evil" ones.

Many of us are sorely aware of the cost of our behaviors, but we are made to feel powerless. We are like cogs in the huge machine of a capitalist economic system that alienates us and turns us into separate parts and commodities. Political systems working within such an economic system legalize and institutionalize security for a small number of people who control the majority of the resources, while the large majority of people live in poverty and despair. Rules of the jungle have been overtly and covertly enforced through laws and reinforced through cultural hegemony.

Nihilism, Alienation, and Cynicism

In our society, we are being transformed by the capitalist economy as well as by technology. In a highly individualistic and mechanistic society, we are estranged from our true nature as spontaneously connected and loving beings. We put fences around ourselves; parents part ways with little concern for the well-being of their young children. Millions of people resort to drugs for consolation. We find it difficult to trust each other, consciously or unconsciously guarding ourselves as if others are enemies; we teach our children to be wary of strangers and panic as soon as our children are out of sight. Politicians treat other parties as opponents, employing all kinds of tactics to attack the other party. Many of us adopt a critical attitude toward issues and problems while we know a constructive and loving attitude will present us with much better solutions. We forget to ask, "What little things can we do every day to make the world a little bit better?"

Moral Breakdown

In a relativist mindset of moral values, we have created huge moral vacuums in schools and society. Wrong doings are often justified as right moves, as they are coined in a legal framework. For example, big corporations swindle billions of dollars out of the pockets of individual investors; CEOs pay themselves hundreds of millions of dollars while thousands of their workers are laid off or paid a meager salary on which a family can barely survive. Movies glorify violence, heralding "heroes" who kill ruthlessly, and popular songs twist the psyche of young people toward cynicism and violence. Children are bathed in commercials from an early age, conditioned to long for instant gratification of their desires, and government officials use their positions to reap personal gains, which leads to rampant corruption around the world. Wealthy countries waste a huge amount of food and resources while millions of people in poor countries are starving. We have created a world "everyone is for himself or herself," and that "might equals strength."

We have separated the practice of moral virtues in our daily life from the pursuit of truth in all domains of our life. Philosophy is no longer for ordinary people, and studies of ethics have become endless technical, complex arguments. We divide our life into private and public domains, and many immoral acts are considered no one else's business because they belong to the "private domain." We embrace the philosophy of scholars who divide us into different "races" or "civilizations" and ignore those people who unite and connect us through the power of their love and wisdom. Acting morally is turned into a free choice rather than a necessity.

Spiritual Conflicts and Breakdown

Wars have been waged and violence has been committed in the name of religions. Religious groups proclaim the superiority of their own religion and deities over those of others, hence breeding intolerance and exclusion. Religious conflicts and misunderstandings add new violence to old hatred, making it increasingly more difficult for rivals to come together and become reconciled. Cultures and religions, although sharing many similarities, clash. Zealous believers in one religion have little or no tolerance for those of another religion. Fear and vengeance are preached; religious teaching affirms irreconcilable differences among people (we are the children of God, and others are evil people, for example). In religious organizations, hierarchy and rituals are often stressed over the equality of men and women, and over searching for self and internal enlightenment.

DEBUNKING THE RATIONALISTIC
POSITIVISTIC PARADIGM

In modern science, the human spirit, mind, and body are posited to be separate. We believe we can seek knowledge by engaging only our mind but not our heart and soul as a whole. We study the world by using a reductionist approach; that is, the whole is broken into parts that are understood as separated entities. The goal of science is to achieve efficiency, validity, and evidence-based knowledge. Scientists see the world as "out there" and believe it must be studied objectively and unemotionally so that all "human factors" are eliminated.

In the process of scientific development, one issue has become outstanding: We focus so much on parts, we see the world as elements to be divided into ever smaller parts to study, that we have forgotten the whole. We forget to posit ourselves in the context of our global community, in the ecosystem of our Mother Earth and the universe. While we invent more effective and more powerful machines to manipulate the world, we have not developed a corresponding global moral ethic of acting responsibly and wisely, hence our ecological home is in greater danger than ever of a total breakdown.

DEBUNKING THE NOTION OF DEVELOPMENT

Insatiable desire for "development" and "growth" has led to relentless exploitation of the Mother Earth (Hicks, 1988). Modernization features individualism and rationalism, which see nature as something to be subdued and controlled. The relationship between humankind and nature has become that of plundering and unlimited manipulation. Wars break out and conflicts arise as a result of the competition to control resources and maintain superior power.

Eastern and Western sages and mystics, through deep meditation and intense search for enlightenment, have experienced the profound harmony among forces and the love energy undergirding the universe. Through directly experiencing the force working in our life and nature, their understanding of the place of the humankind goes beyond the boundary of the human environment. Their outlook on the cosmos and their wisdom and knowledge reveal that humans cocreate with a complexly interconnected universe while at the same time we depend on and support the existence of other species and things. They reveal that we are moving in a yoga with the cosmos, that destructive behaviors cause destruction, and positive relationships assure survival and sustainability.

Modern science posits that humankind occupies a central position in the cosmos, and humankind's function is to discover, occupy, and take advantage of things that are useful to us. The wisdom of native and indigenous people, who see spirits and interconnections in all existences in the universe, is downplayed, neglected, or even denigrated as "barbaric and uncivilized." Since the French Revolution and the Renaissance, while human beings have broken free from religious domination, the role of human beings has been highly exaggerated. It has been stressed that the goal of the human society is to follow a development model that goes from lower to higher level, from smaller to larger scale, from the traditional to the modern, from rural to urban, and from smaller to larger amounts of production and consumption. Our way of thinking has changed from subjective to objective, and education has switched its priority for moral learning and character formation to "learning skills and knowledge" that answer market needs. To sum up, the model that dominates social development and educational studies stresses economic efficiency and development and pays insufficient attention to the development of students as whole persons.

In current academic paradigm, we have operated on rational, dualist epistemologies. Research in science and social sciences emphasizes our separate identity as individuals or groups, creating disconnection rather than connection and wholeness.

It is high time that we emphasize our oneness with the universe. One serious problem today is that we often fail to see ourselves as existentially connected with the environment. We are protected from cold and heat, from rain or sunshine. We have lost the perennial wisdom about how nature works and how dependent we are on our environment. New paradigms must be found to transcend the limitations in social and educational theories. Functional theories, by emphasizing differentiation, conflict theory, by stressing our struggle for power and resources, and critical theory, by looking at hegemony, fail to connect us with each other and with the universe. To build a community from society and nature with common aspirations, to learn to coexist as a species, it is time we work on our commonality rather than insisting on our separation.

Epistemologically, we should place ourselves in the vast universe and cultivate a perspective on our coexistence that includes knowing intellectually, emotionally, morally, spiritually, and ecologically our connections with the souls of all existences. We should consider the universe our origin as well as our final home and refuge. A sense of common destiny should engender a caring and kind heart and a sense of responsibility toward everything.

In social science, the anthropocentric view in developmental theories posits that human beings are in the center of the universe, are superior to all other existences, and have the right to subject all species on Earth out of human greed. We are even planning wars in space so that we can maintain our superiority. We deem ourselves rational beings while all other species are "non-thinking," "non-feeling," hence inferior to us. Destructive competitiveness in our societies has gravely intensified our exploitation of Mother Earth. Fighting for resources has led to wars, conflicts, and the pollution and destruction of our environment. As Martin Luther King urges,

Somehow we must transform the dynamics of the world power struggle from the nuclear arms race, which no one can win, to a creative contest to harness man's genius for the purpose of making peace and prosperity a reality for all the nations of the world. In short, we must shift the arm race into a "peace race." (King, 1967a)

DEBUNKING THE THEORY OF CIVILIZATION CLASHES

Since the publication of Samuel Huntington's book *The Clash of Civilizations and Remaking of World Order* (1996), leaders and scholars have carried on a discourse that stresses cultural differences as the source of global conflicts, intolerance, competitions, and power struggles. Huntington says,

Spurred by modernization, global politics is being reconfigured along cultural lines. People and countries with similar culture are coming together. Peoples and countries with different cultures are coming apart. Alignments defined by ideology and superpower relations are giving way to alignment by culture and civilization. Political boundaries increasingly are redrawn to coincide with cultural ones: ethnic, religious, and civilizational. Cultural communities are replacing Cold War blocs, and the fault lines between civilizations are becoming the central lines of conflict in global politics. (1996, p. 125)

Such a discourse assumes that human division is greater than its unity, and that huge groups of people can be lumped together and categorized and dichotomized as "civilizations" that have irreconcilable differences with others, based on their culture, history, and beliefs. Huntington fails to consider the fact that we are, more importantly, a human species with many more similarities than differences. People of different civilizations share a profound concern for peace and harmony; parents of all countries have profound love for their children; conscientious people from all over the world long for social equality and justice. All people want to be loved and respected; all people dislike violence. The notion that the world's civilizations must clash only creates more divisions and generates more misunderstandings, rather than helping us find common solutions to challenges facing all humanity.

AWAKENING THE COLLECTIVE CONSCIOUSNESS

Our survival and prosperity require a collective awakening and a deep transformation. We can no longer operate on the notion of separation; it is time we take our destiny into our hands by denouncing all forms of violence, by bringing loving kindness into our society and education. We must reimagine education and cultivate a new discourse in education, in a fundamental and grand way, on how we want to live as a human race.

Our collective will carries tremendous power. It can move mountains. Our reality first and foremost comes from our thoughts, which are the seeds for birthing a new reality. From thoughts to our speech, and finally to actions, we as a human race can change our reality for a much better future. This realization should empower us to see that if each one of us does our bit to make our world a better place, soon we will find we are living in a pleasantly different world. We will have eternal peace if we collectively say a resounding "No!" to any forms of violence, intolerance, hatred, injustices, and inequalities. To do this, we need to have a collective awakening; we need to fill our hearts with love. We need people whose acts and words are integrated. Our hearts and souls need to be expanded to embrace all humanity and all species on Earth as our beloved family. Through such a universal loving kindness, we can establish a set of common core values that emphasize our rights and responsibilities to ourselves as well as to each other and to the ecosystem. This great expansion of our mindset and our hearts and souls can be nurtured only by unconditional love for all beings and all existences as divine souls. We are all equal and valuable at the soul's level, regardless of our current status. As the global world is being linked like a neighborhood through information technology, we can likewise connect our hearts and souls as a beloved global family. We need to love and forgive unconditionally to have a fresh start for a new world, a world that is loving, peaceful, and sustainable. This is a grand challenge facing all individuals and all societies in the 21st century.

LOVE AS THE GLOBAL AND
UNIVERSAL ETHIC AND LANGUAGE

In the face of the seemingly endless conflicts and misunderstandings plaguing the human race, philosophers and mystics have long searched for a "universal characteristic" that can connect all minds and hearts (Eco 1997), for a global ethic (Kung 1991), for the creation of a "secondary language" with which the human race can communicate in spite of their differences in culture, languages, and religions (Lee 2000). However, without first embracing universal love, that is, love for all people and existences as our beloved brothers and sisters, many efforts will remain superficial and unsustainable. It is loving others as we love ourselves that generates global respect, understanding, community, peace, and harmony—*love is the true motive and energy for peace*. Cultivating such a love for others would let us cut through our differences and estrangement and connect us as a peaceful race, since "violence never touches love" (Plato 1986).

SCHOOL REFORMS TODAY: WHERE ARE WE HEADING?

Education is first and foremost the engine for making new beings. It has the power of transforming our world by teaching young people that our core essence entails the full equality of all human beings and all existences, that all forms of life come from the same source, created with divine sparks. Education is a calling to teach people to live interdependently with a deep respect for all. It is endowed with the task of giving meaning and the joy of life to souls that are searching for love and enlightenment.

In our society and in our school system today, there is a great neglect of the paramount challenges we are facing in the world: How can our schools become the pivotal force in the construction of global, long-lasting peace? Since the mid-1980s, school reforms have dodged the critical questions: What do we want to do as a human race to solve the critical problems we are facing today? How do schools and societies need to be transformed to ensure our collective survival in the 21st century?

Clearly, we are destined to initiate new reforms that are accompanied by a vision for a grand future for the human race and Mother Earth. The goal of education must change from emphasizing only intellectual development to the holistic, integrated development of students' moral, emotional, ecological, and spiritual capabilities; we must educate our children to be kind and compassionate, to be sensitive and caring. These qualities are not secondary, but they are to be the *top priorities of education* in schools in the 21st century. Our future citizens need to be equipped with the know-how to deal with life challenges and to transcend hatred through the cultivation of a universal, unconditional love for all. We should learn to shorten the distance between what we aspire to—our desire and our actions for a peaceful, harmonious world—and what we are doing daily in the classroom.

Underneath our differences in skin color, sex, cultural background, and beliefs is a divine spark that shines in our souls. Our material possessions have little to do with our soul's achievement. What matters is how we use our soul force—we are challenged as educators in the new millennium to change our thoughts, speeches, and actions to light up the world with the light of love.

The challenge is thus for the institution of education to undergo a paradigm shift to emphasize the heart and soul of students. Today, "many classrooms are spiritually empty, not by accident, but by design" (Kessler 2000, p. xii). It is commonplace for teachers to suppress their students' expression or

exploration of their own beliefs, longings, or search for a spiritually meaningful experience (p. xiv). Kessler observes,

> When schools systematically exclude heart and soul, students in growing num-
> bers become depressed, attempt suicide, or succumb to eating disorders and sub-
> stance abuse. Students struggle to find their motivation to learn to stay in school,
> or to keep their attention on what is before them. And straight-A students drive
> their BMWs on their way to shooting fellow students and attempting to inciner-
> ate their school with explosives. (2000, p. xii)

To light up our world with love, we need to cultivate students to have big
hearts, to embrace all people, all species, and all existences in the universe as
our beloved brothers and sisters. We need to help our students open their divine eyes to see the divine sparks in all people and existences; we need to intensively nurture wisdom more than just intellect, to elevate their spirits. Students must find meaning in their learning and living.

Our education system is ripe for a major shift from being a mechanistic,
factory-style institution to being a place for learning and nurturing love, the
primordial force that nourishes life and gives us joy. Our life has a purpose,
and education cannot be deemed successful at enriching the meaning of our
students' lives unless knowledge is connected with wisdom. Students need
to learn how to live a life through giving and receiving love. We as educators must have a grand vision: What do we want the world to become
through the education of our younger generation? Painting a vivid picture
of a loving, peaceful, harmonious, and sustainable world embarks us on the
journey to search for strategies and build up courage to change our world
for the better. We will stop feeling powerless when we see violence raging
around the world. As we start to integrate love into every aspect of our lives,
we will begin to turn ourselves into workers of peace in our schools, communities, and society; a new world is already beckoning to us on the new
horizon.

For changes to take place, a paradigm shift will not occur out there; rather,
it must happen right here in our hearts. We do not need to wait for years of
debates before we can come to the conclusion that change is needed. We do
not need authorities to tell us what the current priority is. We can start at this
moment. A kind thought, a caring gesture, a small sum of money donated, an
article published, a group formed—these acts bring changes right away. Gi-
ant steps start from small; what it takes is to act *now*.

The universe is a holographic entity. We as individuals reflect the whole of
the universe. We are a part of the universe, and the universe is a part of us. The
underlying interconnectedness of all existences can be directly experienced
once we open our spiritual eyes and cultivate deep spiritual sensitivity through

nurturing a profound, compassionate love for all. We are an open system in a perpetual exchange of energies and spirits with all other existences. We figuratively and literally depend on each other for survival. The book *The Last Hours of Ancient Sunlight* (Hartmann 1999) vividly describes the mutual dependence between humans and trees: Our trees "inhale" carbon dioxide from our atmosphere and use the energy of sunlight to drive a chemical reaction in their leaves called photosynthesis. In the process of manufacturing carbohydrates, oxygen is "exhaled" as a waste gas by the plants. Meanwhile, human beings inhale the oxygen as vital nutrients and exhale carbon dioxide as waste, nutrition for plants again. Hence, a cycle of life support is formed. There are many other examples one can cite to illustrate that the well-being of humans is related to that of other species in the ecosystem, and vice versa.

The universe is not chaotic and mechanical. The universe is conscious. It is consciously creating life out of love-energy. Opening our spiritual eyes and listening to our souls, we will be able to feel and hear the heartbeat of all existences—be they flowers, water, clouds, birds, mountains, trees— and we can feel that they are all instruments playing a compassionate and joyful song of love. From a scientific perspective, they are all constantly emitting light and electromagnetic energy, which travel out into space and share with all that exists (Tompkins and Bird 1989; Goodman 1979). When we are in tune with this cosmic energy, a tremendous sense of unity will transform us. A heart knowing the music of love and joy of the whole universe cannot hate anymore. Enlightened masters in world religions and culture, who have repeatedly demonstrated their unfailing love to us, throughout history have urged us to take the whole world and the universe into our concept of family.

People who have known the great love have deep concern for social equality and justice. They want to see that all people and other existences are treated with dignity and love. They become more tolerant, more embracing; they have deep compassion for all people and are always ready to reach out to help, support, and glorify others. It is toward this goal that we should reimagine the roles and functions of education in the 21st century.

PARADIGM CHANGE IN THE 21st CENTURY

Our world is hugely divided by the gulf of misunderstanding and the lack of respect for each other. Information technology has shortened time and distance, making instant communication possible, but the hearts and minds of people are not being intimately connected yet. Instead, gulfs between different interests and powers have prevented us from developing a consensus as to what kind of world we want to build in the 21st century. Discussion about the clashes of civilization takes over the heart-to-heart talk among peoples and nations about forming a global ethic for our common survival and prosperity. We fail to see that the greatest dangers in our world are walls established between hearts and souls, and that we can never bring down the walls through flaunting our military might and national arrogance.

It is critically important that as a human race we act *now* to address how we can educate our younger generation to live in the 21st century as a beloved community, a global family, in harmony with nature, and with a good understanding of life's meaning and purpose, to build a world of love and peace for all.

All these efforts call for a drastic paradigm shift that will give us new perspectives, new outlooks, new discoveries, new hopes. Thomas Kuhn (1996) talks about scientific paradigm change:

> Examining the record of past research from the vantage of contemporary historiography, the historians of science may be tempted to exclaim that when paradigms change, the world adopts new instruments and looks in new places. Even more important, during revolutions scientists see new and different things when looking with familiar instruments in places they have looked before. It is rather as if the professional community had been suddenly transported to another planet where familiar objects are seen in a different light and are joined by unfamiliar ones as well. . . . We may want to say after a revolution scientists are responding to a different world. (p. 111)

We can have a similar impact with a paradigm shift in our understanding of the basic guiding principles for humanity. The new paradigm is to be one based on love and interconnectedness, one that can help us build a world of peace and harmony. In education, we should institutionalize our efforts to socialize students into loving and caring beings. The paradigm shift is simple once we see that it is love, not hatred, that works for our world! This shift will powerfully change the way we live and act to make the world peaceful and sustainable.

Chapter Two

The Centrality of Love in Human Society and the Universe

To educate our future global residents to be kinder and wiser, a new philosophy of education and a new epistemology must be formed, which should be based on the centrality of love. The main proposition I am putting forward here is that we are by nature loving and kind beings, and this quality is central to our essence as global and universal citizens. Education should acknowledge and cultivate this propensity and potential in all of our children.

LOVE IS THE ESSENCE OF OUR BEING AND THE UNIVERSE

Love is the underlying force and energy that enables all existences to have life and to thrive. It is the universal energy that connects souls and hearts. The deepest kind of love is unconditional love, which gives without seeking reward. Spontaneously outflowing and giving, it is like the sun and the moon shining their light to Earth, nurturing all forms of life on earth without any expectation of return. Because they do not ask for return, the giving is unconditional and of the truest kind. Lao Zi, a Chinese sage, praises the virtue of water as the highest form of virtue, for water nurtures all forms of life without asking for return. Water is always willing to remain in lowly places. It is precisely because of this virtue that water fills up the valleys and gaps and eventually enlarges itself to become lakes, seas, and oceans of great vastness and immense power.

We come to life through the love of our parents. Our parents demonstrate the most unconditional kind of love: No matter how much hardship they have to go through, they never fail to nurture their children with love; they are willing to sacrifice a great deal so that their children live a better life than they have had. They always hold out a loving hand when their children return home, even though some terrible mistakes may have been made. Likewise, animals, birds, and even plants demonstrate similar instincts of love that enable them to nurture their children's lives. Under the roof of my house, there used to be a nest. For several years, a robin couple would come to raise their family in it in spring. The mother bird patiently sat in her nest, hour after hour, day after day, and the father bird stood guard nearby, watching in love and caution and fetching food for the mother. When the young birds hatched, the mother bird tirelessly flew back and forth to search for food for her children. No one educated her to do this; *it was built into her essence to love her children*. One can say that without the love and care of others, no individuals or species can survive. Basically, we are built to love to ensure our collective survival.

The planet Earth is another great example of selfless giving. The fertile soil of Mother Earth provides nutrition for plants and produces food for animals and human beings. She never fails to give. Giving is her nature. Without the nutrition of love from Mother Earth, plants will dwindle, and animals and humans will not survive. Opening our spiritual eyes and listening with our spiritual ears, we will find experientially that the universe itself is a song of love. The exquisite designs of many flowers often make us wonder if they are not created from a heart of sheer love, what could they be. The colors, the shapes, the fragrances of flowers are incredibly diverse, yet they are perfectly harmonious. In a similar manner, oceans and lands form a loving relationship. Evaporation of the ocean forms clouds that flow inland and send fresh water down to the land; rivers collect the water and send it back to sea. These evidences demonstrate that all forms of life and all existences are unconditionally, selflessly engaged in a supportive relationship, singing a tune of love, through beauties in their own right, making the universe an immensely colorful, bountiful, and beautiful grand-scale symphony.

We have used the "reasoning" power of the mind to argue about the principles of the universe and life, seeing the universe as only a mechanical system without souls and hearts, no designs or morals, no love or joy. To know the truth of the universe more fully, we need to use our feelings, as "feeling is the language of the soul" (Walsh 1995, p. 3). We need to open the "eye of the heart" (Tutu 2004). Through our feelings, we experience the universe as alive and become part of its dynamic living force. Love is the grandest feeling we have for each other, for the universe and life.

THE ACT OF LOVE

What is love? There may be endless answers to this question. In this book, love is defined as the very essence of our existence. It is a great sense of oneness, nonseparation, all-inclusion, as exemplified by such attributes as compassion, respect, kindness, forgiveness, care, service, and so on. Love is inherent in our soul's purpose, which seeks joy and fulfillment through experiencing love. Simultaneously, love is the permeating energy that enables all people and all existences to connect with and support each other. It is the deepest instinct, allowing all that exists to feel unity and oneness, and to maintain the survival and balance of life and the universe.

Love is deeply embedded in us. Major religions in the world teach us that we all have boundless love within us, but it is hidden under layers of dust and held back by barriers such as fear and anger. Love is the ability of the soul to fill our hearts with joy and meaning. With love, relationships sustain, families are happy, and communities are welcoming places. Teachers in all major religions have lauded love as the most important of all human capacities (Walsh 1999, p. 75).

We have the capacity to lead loving lives. Translated into daily living, love is defined as our loving intention, loving speech, loving acts. It means deep concern for all lives and existences as divine souls. It means being able to see others as ourselves. It means taking the stand of others and seeing our humanity in all circumstances. Love is crucial in the family, in the workplace, in political circles, in relations between countries, and in the bond between humanity and nature. With this love, we foster a deep belief in equality for all and uphold a sincere and profound respect for all beings regardless of differences in cultural background, race, class, gender, or ethnicity. Thus, the love I am talking about has no conditions attached and knows no boundaries.

Harboring love for all gives birth to a heart of great compassion, one that can embrace the whole of humanity and all existences in the universe. A spirit guided by love sees all human beings and all existences as from the same source, inseparable and equal, each carrying a divine light that makes the universe a shining place.

LOVE IS JOY; LOVE IS PEACE AND HARMONY

Love is joy. Those who have love in their hearts know joy in life. Life without love is like a desert. Parents experience tremendous, deep joy through loving their children; we experience joy through giving love and receiving love. Love is warmth, acceptance, harmony, peace, fulfillment, brightness, light, and meaningful existence.

Love is reflected in such qualities as giving, caring, respect, forgiveness, service, understanding, and compassion. It is love that forms a network of mutual support in human life and in the ecological world. At the deepest level, love connects hearts and souls of all people and existences. Through love we see beauty in all people and existences. This is where compassion springs from and flows like an endless fountain.

Abundant scientific research supports the argument that love is a positive energy that nurtures the growth and well-being of all life forms. Even loving intentions cure. For example, scientific experiments show that expressing good wishes in one's heart (such as through prayer) can in reality help patients significantly improve their health (Dossey 1993). Research finds that not only human beings thrive on love, even plants need love as nutrition (Tompkins and Bird 1973). It is possible that human life, and in fact the whole universe, is created for the purpose of sharing and experiencing love (Eadie 1992). Love carries great power, for only with the power of love can we transcend hatred. Only love can help us nurture a universal sisterhood and brotherhood in its truest sense, as has been powerfully argued by Mahatma Gandhi (Kripalani 2001) and Martin Luther King Jr. (Ayres 1993).

SPIRITUALITY AND SCIENCE CROSSROADS

Scientific discovery in quantum physics is affirming the Eastern spiritual teaching of life's interconnectedness. Quantum physics finds that we are not living only in a physical world where things and events are separate entities; instead, there is an underlying interconnectedness among all existences in the universe. Our emotions and feelings are not "obstacles" to scientific discovery, but they have everything to do with the very findings we want to achieve (Capra 2000).

Researchers have also found that plants have feelings. Even soils have intelligence (Tompkins and Bird 1989). When a person threatens to burn a planet's leaves, detective tools found that plants respond violently, whereas loving touch and emotions receive corresponding responses from plants (Tompkins and Bird 1973). This corresponds with teachings in Eastern religions and Native American spirituality that all existences are conscious, and all live with emotions and feelings. They all have spirits.

WHAT IS LOVE? EXPANDING OUR UNDERSTANDING

Love is furthermore a state of being. It requires us to be unconditionally kind and forgiving toward each other. Love leads to a lifestyle in which a person harbors kind intentions, speaks kind words, and does kind deeds at all times. A loving person knows the deep secret of reciprocity. It is shown in young people harboring deep respect for the elderly, and elderly people maintaining great affection for the young. Teachers not only teach but also shine hope and care on students, and in return the students do what the teacher expects them to do. This reciprocal relationship is beyond calculation and is the act of true giving. It is here that the soul finds its joy.

In the world's spiritual traditions and religions, love is the primary theme. Love is vital for spiritual growth and for improving our health and longevity. Mystical teachings emphasize harboring unconditional love as a must for anyone who aspires to achieve a high level of spiritual development and even immortality (such as is evidenced in Taoism, Christianity, and Buddhism). Without the cultivation of a compassionate heart for all beings and existences, one cannot expect to achieve a high level of spiritual development. Because we are by nature loving beings, inflicting harm to others causes inner suffering (of the soul) and depletion of energy. We will eventually suffer the pain we have inflicted on others (this is the key belief in karma in Buddhism and Taoism and other mystical traditions).

Love is the primordial energy and the fundamental element that connects and sustains, and that attracts and circulates. Our acts that are love based and care based generate loving energy, which ripples out to the world and returns to the giver; likewise, anger and hatred generate negative energy that causes sufferings in others, and that eventually circles back to the one who inflicts pain on others.

Love is nonviolence. It is giving life rather than taking life or hurting life. Only when we as a human race are fully committed to love-based nonviolence can we find a way out of our current crises. Gandhi and King have said eloquently that only through nonviolence can we find the final solution to human predicament. The "eye for an eye" mentality must be replaced by unconditional forgiveness and reconciliation. As King says,

> Nonviolence is the answer to the crucial political and moral questions of our time: the need for man to overcome oppression and violence without resorting to oppression and violence. Man must evolve for all human conflict a method which rejects revenge, aggression and retaliation. The foundation of such a method is love. (King 1964)

LOVE HAS BEEN THE HUMAN QUEST

Great teachers have impacted the human race tremendously by urging us to practice unconditional love toward each other. This is true of Confucius, Lao Zi, the Buddha, Jesus Christ, Muhammad, Mahatma Gandhi, Martin Luther King Jr., and Mother Teresa, to name just a few. They have won the hearts and souls of people not through the force of weapons, but through the power of love. They have given us love as skills, as tools, as a fundamental mechanism, and as a powerful, practical strategy to effectively resolve our conflicts and problems. For these sages, there is no separation of the self from others, as love connects them all like the iceberg under water; for them, loving others is loving oneself, and vice versa. These teachers become great not because they want to stand above others, but because they give themselves unconditionally to benefit the life of others, making others great beings like themselves.

ONLY LOVE CAN TRANSFORM US TOWARD A HIGHER LEVEL OF FREEDOM

Let us not seek to satisfy our thirst for freedom by drinking from the cup of bitterness and hatred. We must forever conduct our struggle on the high plane of dignity and discipline. We must not allow our creative protest to degenerate into physical violence. Again and again we must rise to the majestic heights of meeting physical force with soul force. (King 1963b)

It is clear that only through the power of love can we realize the dream of equality among all people and all nations. True equality has to spring from the heart, from the outflowing of genuine love for each other. This is the basis of Dr. King's announcement:

I have a dream that one day this nation will rise up and live out the true meaning of its creed: "We hold these truths to be self-evident, that all men are created equal." I have a dream that one day on the red hills of Georgia the sons of former slaves and the sons of former slave owners will be able to sit down together at the table of brotherhood. I have a dream that one day even the state of Mississippi, a state sweltering with the heat of injustice, sweltering with the heat of oppression, will be transformed into an oasis of freedom and justice. I have a dream that my four little children will one day live in a nation where they will not be judged by the color of their skin but by the content of their character. I have a dream today. I have a dream that one day down in Alabama, with its vicious racists, with its governor having his lips dripping with the words of interposition and nullification—one day right there in Alabama little black boys and black girls will be able to join hands with little white boys and white girls as sisters and brothers. (King 1963b)

The love postulated by Martin Luther King Jr. is one of true sisterhood and brotherhood, for in his love, there are no enemies. There are only people who need to understand who they truly are. There are only people who need to communicate and understand each other, who build a dream world not through hatred but through love.

In Lao Zi's description, truly enlightened people are so loving that they never give up on anyone and they return love for hatred. Jesus demonstrates his love by being willing to suffer for all, for he sees others' suffering as his own.

> In the final analysis, love is not this sentimental something that we talk about. It's not merely an emotional something. Love is creative, understanding good-will for all men. It is the refusal to defeat any individual. When you rise to the level of love, of its great beauty and power, you seek only to defeat evil systems. Individuals who happen to be caught up in that system, you love, but you seek to defeat the system. There's something about love that builds up and is creative. There is something about hate that tears down and is destructive. So love your enemies. (King 1957)

LOVE TRANSCENDS ANGER AND HATRED AND ENGENDERS FORGIVENESS

Only through love can we hope to transcend hatred. Hatred is a poisonous emotion that sets our body into chemical reactions that disturb the normal functioning of our body. The Chinese medicinal philosophy sees most ill-nesses as resulting from the blocking of energy by negative emotions. Like-wise, hatred is the poisoning chemical in a society that distorts human rela-tionships and perpetuates human suffering. Love is peace. It is through the power of love that we can create new social structures and new relationships. When we make decisions out of fear, we see others as threats and shut doors that lead to understanding. Hence, to have peace or not is to choose between love and fear (Walsh 1995, p. 19). The South African experience, through the success of the Truth and Reconciliation Commission, demonstrates that when we resort to our ability to love, despite decades of pain and anger brought about by apartheid, we can rekindle the human spirit of brotherhood and sis-terhood through forgiveness and reconciliation, and we can have a new world (Tutu 1999).

LOVE MUST BE EXTENDED TO ALL EXISTENCES

The love I am talking about here is not only love for humankind, but love for all existences. This Love is based on our oneness with All. As many re-ligions and cultures inform us, all existences come from the same source, and it is this oneness that enables us, especially children, to feel the inner heart of and to develop positive emotions toward animals and plants and all that exists.

We are experiencing more irregular weather conditions and receive warnings of all kinds about the breaking down of the balance of our climate and natural environment. Thomas Berry somberly states,

> If the earth does grow inhospitable toward human presence, it is primarily because we have lost our sense of courtesy toward the earth and its inhabitants, our sense of gratitude, our willingness to recognize the sacred character of habitat, our capacity for the awesome, for the numinous quality of every earthly reality. We have even forgotten our primordial capacity for language at the elementary level of song and dance, wherein we share our existence with the animals and with all natural phenomena. (1988, p. 2)

Berry talks about a common language, a capacity to care for each other and an intensive sharing with the natural world. However, we seldom enter the worlds of animals with empathy; instead, we have drawn them into our context in some subservient way, often in a derogatory way.

Our love should extend to plants, animals, birds, mountains, water—in a word, all existences. In them we see our insignificance and become humbled. Sensitive hearts and eyes need to be cultivated not only to see the beauty of nature but also reach a deep realization that we can never "own" or "possess" nature; rather, we can only be part of nature, and our only choice is to learn to live in harmony with nature. Our concept of family should be extended to take in animals, plants, and all existences. When we do this, we live in great communion with all. As Berry puts it:

> We have before us the question not simply of physical survival, but of survival in a human mode of being, survival and development into intelligent, affectionate, imaginative persons thoroughly enjoying the universe about us, living in profound communion with one another and with some significant capacities to express ourselves in our literature and creative arts. It is a question of interior richness within our own personalities, of shared understanding with others, and of a concern that reaches out to all the living and nonliving beings of the earth, and in some manner out to the distant stars in the heavens. (Berry 1988, p. 37)

LOVE AND INTELLIGENCE

We cannot be intelligent without having in our heart profound love for all beings and existences. Krishnamurti puts it very powerfully:

> When one comprehends the nature of love, when one has that quality of the mind in the heart, that is intelligence. Intelligence is a comprehension or discovery of what love is. One might be very adept in one's studies, and in one's

work, capable of arguing with much aptitude and rationality, but that is not intelligence. Intelligence goes hand in hand with love and compassion; and a person, as a separate individual, cannot come to that intelligence. (cited in Nava 2001, p. 47)

Love as intelligence leads us to become responsible, moral, and spiritual beings. Love as intelligence is the guiding light that gives our intellect direction. These two combined form true intelligence.

LOVE AND EGO

Embracing universal love leads to the shrinking and eventually letting go of our ego. Our ego posits our selves as the center of attention and as beings separate from all that exists. Letting go of ego is the precondition to reaching out and having compassion, to emptying ourselves of jealousy and merging with the universe's will for all.

Our culture and education has called for the building of a strong ego. In our culture, the value of our life is pinned to our forming a strong self-centered ego and striving for personal success. In the excessive stress of individualism, the self is often lifted above the collective. Yet, as world's great religions teach us, we can never become an ocean of love without giving up our self-centeredness and ethnocentric views. When we are able to see all existences as equal, we let go of clinging to self-importance and become capable of what Buddhism and Taoism say is the breaking down of our attachment to our sense of self. The blending of the meaning and purpose of self with the larger Self is the first step to learning about truth in the universe—that is, there is no separation of souls, and we are all one. We and all existences are from the same source, formed of the same materials, and our souls and spirits are interconnected.

LOVE AS OUR PLANETARY COLLECTIVE CONSCIOUSNESS

Realizing that all life comes from love, we need to develop universal love as our planetary collective consciousness. It is a challenge for us all to stop hatred and anger and work on our peaceful and ecologically responsible existence. With love as our collective consciousness, we will see very clearly that we have a simple and straightforward solution to our problems. If we align our consciousness with love, if we treat each other as our loving brothers and sisters, we will not have wars; we will not have debilitating poverty; and we will have a balanced and harmonious environment. We can let go of political

bickering and reshape our reality and future. Hence, forming a planetary consciousness based on love is the foundation for stopping all fighting, beginning
healing, reconciliation, and the building of full understanding and acceptance
of each other.

LOVE AND EQUALITY

Political and economic systems in our world are essentially still operating on the
notion of survival of the fittest, and thus it is legally protected and morally ac-
ceptable for some people to possess a huge amount of wealth while many others
struggle on the brink of hunger and starvation. Human beings have been placed
in unequal social categories based on what they own, their birth, gender, race,
ethnicity, religion, and other factors irrelevant to our true essence as equal souls.
The realization of our nature as souls in search of enlightenment through love
would enable us to see beyond our "differences" and realize that the injustices
in our society deprive the rich as well as the poor, for rich people would know
in their souls, as spiritual beings, that they are taking from their brothers and sisters, whose suffering is deep down also their own suffering. Knowing that the
soul's highest purpose is to experience love, our life can be an engagement in
both giving and receiving it. We will be in pain if we have not done enough for
each other as individuals and as a race.

CONCLUSION

This chapter deconstructs the notion of otherness, the illusion that we are separated from each other and from our environment. It posits that love is our
very essence, and it is also the essence of the whole universe.

Since the 1990s, people have discussed the forming of a global ethic (Kung
1991) that would enable us to transcend our religious, cultural differences.
Some have discussed the formation of a "second language" that would enable
humankind to build consensus on critical issues facing us (Lee 2000). Organizations and individuals have been working hard to bring people together
and build peace. We need to do more. We need to fundamentally build a culture of love as a human planetary consciousness. Our policies and strategies
for the future should stem from this consciousness. Hence, love should be our
global ethic, and love should be the language we use to communicate with
each other, finding common ground, learning to reconcile and reconnect.
Only through loving each other unconditionally can we build a kingdom of
peace and joy on earth.

Chapter Three

Reconstructing School for Love

Education should cultivate a "deep inner sense of personal responsibility for the world" (Walsh 1995, p. 37). In this light, 21st century education is ready to undergo a dramatic shift from schools based on an efficiency model to that of school for love. In such a school, school goals, curriculum, and teacher-student relationships should be transformed to make children learning to love and care the central theme of education. Children are loving creatures; parents derive great joy from child-rearing because children seem to be generators of love. Their smiles, their coo-cooing, and their ways of expression convey unspeakable loving feeling for parents. *Children are born with the energy and ability to love.* In this regard, schools should start with affirming children's good nature and propensities to love, care, respect, and connect with all beings and creations in the universe. A new pedagogy needs to be put in place that sees school as the site for teaching love for family, community, the global world, and all existences in the universe. Education should empower students with habits and skills to bring peace and joy to their own lives and to others' lives.

Synchronistic efforts are required when leaders, parents, and educators redefine excellence and success in education and life; policy makers should consider instituting mechanisms that ensure love, kindness, and compassion will prevail in every aspect of young people's experience. School for love is an environment that provides students the daily experience of working cooperatively and building bridges of understanding and respect. In all, school for love aims to help students form strong values and habits as loving people who are provided with an abundance of opportunities to experience the joy and power of love, and who learn how to transform our world through practicing universal love and unconditional forgiveness.

CURRENT SCHOOLING MODEL: AN EFFICIENCY MODEL

The education that we experience today has been stripped of its former moral dimensions, soulful meaning, and deep ecological understanding in favor of the methodological application of skill development and cognitive training. The honoring of soul, creativity, spontaneity, and play has given way to an almost complete monopoly of practical skill-based knowledge designed to weed out the dreamers and to ensure the perpetuation of the modern technologically oriented world. The goal of most of modern education is to define all aspects of human teaching and learning to such a precise degree that with technical proficiency education can be totally controlled from entrance to exit by the vested interests of the modern industrial-technocratic-political complex. This conceptual orientation has become so prevalent in modern education that the only real opportunity for deep holistic learning is when one exits the system intentionally or by accident or through failure (Cajete 1999, p. 175).

Worldwide, education is perceived and used as a tool for national economic development. Government documents reveal the prevailing rationale that as our world is moving toward globalization, education and science must be used to enhance a country's competitive edge. Educational excellence helps maintain the power and advantage of a country. Although outcries for students' holistic development are heard around the world, the notion of education for training "human capital," for increasing national power and economic growth, occupies an overriding position in policy making.

Education is also being used to justify social inequality and reinforce the exploitation of the rich over the poor in the framework of capitalist economic system. Exclusive elite schools and the stratification of children through tracking segregate children into different learning opportunities, giving them vastly different chances in life. Reflecting the demands of the capitalist economy, schools focus on training individuals to be passive beings who obey authorities without engaging in independent and critical thinking. The definition of success as an individual endeavor has diminished the sense of collective well-being, and passion for the common good is often overridden by pragmatic choices that give one immediate monetary or professional benefits. The brightest talents are attracted to the game of competition, and money-driven motives push individuals to do things regardless of consequences, the worst case being the competition to design the deadliest weapons of mass destruction with those involved feeling no sense of guilt. Further covering up the unequal nature of contemporary education under the notion of "meritocracy," schools have served to justify inequity based on class, gender, race, and other factors; when the disadvantaged don't make it in education and life, it is seen as the victims' fault, or simply their lack of luck.

The drive for constructing a science of education based on the scientific research model objectifies the role of education. One core assumption of scientific research is objectivity. This presumes that the stakeholders in education are to be studied as objects, while emotions, feelings, and moral values are marginalized or seriously devalued. Students' inner well-being is presumed to be a private and subjective domain, which is to remain outside the realm of responsibility of education. Hence, for many students, "when things go bad in their lives, there's nothing to fall back on and also there's no limit to their behavior" ("Kids who kill," 1999, cited in Kessler 2000, p. xi).

Such a mechanistic efficiency model has been criticized (Nava 2001); however, as it is based on the social reality of a capitalist economy where human relations are characterized by hierarchy and competition, it has been hard to break free of the model. Further, the established schooling model reinforces social inequalities, for the underlying assumption is that school is a screening mechanism, and students are to be divided into "smart" and "dumb" ones. In this light, the teaching of unconditional love in school has yet to be a systematic and institutionalized practice. A fundamental paradigm change is needed to correct the vast gap in resources, funding, teaching quality, and student academic achievement characterizing most educational systems in the world today.

A NEW SCHOOLING MODEL: SCHOOL FOR LOVE

The gravest challenge of today's education is not efficiency, accountability, high-stake tests, or international competition. The challenge, the foremost task, is the cultivation of universal, unconditional, all-embracing love in the hearts of all students so that they become the builders of a new world—a better world that gives the human race long-lasting peace and all existences on earth a sustainable ecological home. Education should be about the hearts and souls of students. This reasoning has not been in the main discourse of school reform because we have been reacting to social demands on education and we have been held hostage by the dictatorship of a capitalist economic framework that sees grabbing rather than giving as our motivation. Visionary educators need to come to the forefront to shape the discourse that sets us on the path as pioneers in shaping our future.

The reform rhetoric today often points to the dire fact that schools are falling behind international competitors in meeting high standard for learning. School teachers and principals are under tremendous pressure to cram students with more data and facts, turning children from creative learners into robots who regurgitate what has been fed to them. Such a preoccupation driving more than two decades of school reform, engaging the most talented minds, results in insensitivity and powerlessness. When we see international conflicts escalating in the world, when we watch the violence and consumerism that dominate the media and twist the younger generation's minds and hearts, we remain either indifferent or powerless. For those of us who want to make changes, we have been made to believe that we are individuals fighting all our individual battles alone, and that we can do little to effect positive social changes. We have neglected the building of a collective consciousness and our collective ability to be a powerful force in making our society to be truly more compassionate, loving, and peaceful. Confined to the classroom, educators feel restricted in their ability to shift policy priorities, and limited in their vision of themselves as a monumental force of peace and love.

In the 21st century, educators *can and should be* the most important force in nurturing people to adopt universal love as an answer to our challenges. School for love sees love and care as the indispensable capabilities and skills students must cultivate to be global citizens. They are also the core qualities for an excellent teacher to cultivate and maintain. Education in the 21st century should be education for love, with love and through love; we should cultivate not only intelligence but also wisdom. Love is seen not in opposition to intelligence; love is treated as the precondition for and enhancer of intelligence and wisdom. Love is viewed as the foundation of seeing the interconnectedness of all fields of knowledge and achieving a broad and deep understanding of life. Only through cultivating deep compassion and profound love for all can we open our hearts to embrace and learn from all beings and existences. Love is the guiding light of our soul. Through the light we wake up to our human predicament and act as a collective force to turn around crises and meet our gravest challenges.

CENTRAL VALUES OF THE SCHOOL FOR LOVE

Is it that difficult to make education for love the new priority of education in the 21st century? It is not if we wake up to the need for our collective survival and for a peaceful world. This vision is essential for the adjustment of the goals of education.

The school for love is a loving community. Conceptualizing it and turning it into reality first requires transforming ourselves so that we harbor universal love and cultivate compassionate hearts. Advocating education for love requires us to first aspire to a better future for humankind and all existences on Earth. It takes an expanded awareness and a profound understanding of our purpose, of the vital elements that make our lives fulfilling and joyful. Seeing all people and existences as our beloved family is the first requirement for building a loving community in schools and turning schools into school for love.

What would comprise the central values of the school for love? We believe love, compassion, respect, forgiveness, and holistic approaches should be the central values of the school for love.

Love

The love students in the new school learn is not romantic love but does not exclude it. It is love for one's family and friends, and it is love for all people as our family and friends, and for all species and existences on earth as One. Hence, the love students will learn is greater than the self, greater than the circle of family and friends. This love knows no boundaries or limits. It sees all existences as from the same source, as divine sparks of the universe, all made from love. It is a love without ego. It is a love that blends one's life's purpose with that of the whole of humanity, nature, and the universe. This love calls for a great expansion of our awareness of who we are and what we can become.

This love gives rise to students' learning an unconditional acceptance of each and every form of life as equally divine and precious, as beautiful and wonderful. It empowers one to give without thinking of the fruit of one's actions. This love generates experiences of warmth, joy, fulfillment, and happiness for both the receiver and the giver.

Compassion

Compassion is the ability to empathize with others, to feel what others feel, and to care deeply for each other. With compassion, students see people not as "others" or "strangers," but as human beings like themselves who have emotions, feelings, moral aspirations, and spiritual needs. They understand that all people long for love and thrive on love, yearn for understanding and acceptance, cry when family members die, feel hurt when disrespected, suffer in wars and violence as much as we do. Students put their hearts out to feel the suffering, despair, and helplessness of others as our true sisters and brothers. They see that behind external differences, each and every person has a divine soul that makes us conscious beings. As King says very powerfully:

> Here is the true meaning of compassion and nonviolence, when they help us to see the enemy's point of view, to hear his questions, to know his assessment of ourselves. For from his view we may indeed see the basic weakness of our

condition, and if we are mature, we may learn and grow and profit from the wisdom of the brothers who are called the opposition. (King 1967b, p. 29)

Respect

Respect comes from students knowing that each and everyone of us has our divine purpose in life, that ultimately we are all souls in the pursuit of the joy of universal, unconditional love. Respect for all people leads students to treat people with care, as their teachers having something to teach them, either through positive or negative circumstances. It results in students shedding arrogance and placing themselves in humble positions. Respect begets communication, with which students make friends rather than enemies. The warmth generated by genuine respect helps build a supportive community in school.

Forgiveness

Forgiveness is a value that students need to learn for school for love to become a builder of a new world. Students learn that without forgiveness we do not have peace. Genuine forgiveness sets the offender free to begin a new path in life and prevents the buildup of anger and eventual outbreak of violence. Students are informed that hatred poisons our bodies and hearts, while forgiveness brings health and serenity into our lives. With forgiveness, we have the bright prospect of overcoming misunderstanding and being able to work together to effect positive changes in our world.

At another level, students learn that forgiving is first of all to our own benefit. We cannot rest in peace unless we forgive — for forgiveness releases us from negative feelings. Forgiveness requires sensitivity. It is especially important that students think from other people's perspectives. When sometimes they find it very difficult to forgive, students can reflect on what positive lessons they can learn from the experience and be grateful for having an opportunity to learn even greater love, which they did not know they had. Through learning to forgive, no matter how hard, we find that forgiveness is to come; we transcend ourselves and learn to truly love universally and unconditionally. Forgiveness is an essential element in our well-being and in the world's. Hence, students need to learn forgiveness as a serious science and social science, as a life skill, and as a mechanism for renewing and reviving our world.

Holistic Approaches

As educators, we aspire to foster the qualities described above in all our students in a holistic manner. All of them are interconnected. When we have love, we have compassion. When we are compassionate, we can forgive and respect. Love, compassion, respect, and forgiveness are values, traits, qualities, skills, and knowledge all at the same time. They are idealistic as well as practical—they are lofty beliefs as well as essential tools and mechanisms for us to personally live better lives and collectively build a better world.

PEDAGOGY FOR SCHOOL FOR LOVE

Our education should start with affirming children's good nature and propensities to love, care, respect, and connect with all beings and creations in the universe. A new philosophy should be advanced that sees school's primary role as teaching students to love family, community, the world, Mother Earth, and all existences in the universe. Education should empower students with habits and skills to construct harmony in their lives and the world. Teachers' teaching as well as their modeling of unconditional love and compassion is vital for the implementation of a pedagogy for love.

What is a pedagogy of love? It must include methods that are missing in today's education. Because school for love works not only on students' intellect but also on the development of their hearts and souls, besides the traditional teaching strategies and approaches, the pedagogy of love must include reflectiveness, tranquility and silence, humility and simplicity, and direct contact with nature, among other methods.

Reflectiveness

Reflectiveness should be an important part of our teaching approach. We need to build reflectiveness into our teaching plan, with the goals that our students reflect on their life's purpose and become mindful of the intentions, thoughts, and behaviors that affect our environment and create the world we live in. Thus, we share with students our views on important events in our lives; we urge students to reflect on what bring them joy; teachers and students probe questions that have come up in their learning and lives with understanding and thoughtfulness. The classroom is a place for students to explore all questions that touch on life, nature, and the universe. Teachers are respectful of the questions students bring out in different periods of their lives; they encourage students to seek answers from nature, from the inner self, from teachers, parents, books, and their role models. They encourage students to think of themselves as global citizens and residents of Mother Earth and the universe. Students are urged to ask questions and respond to each other's questions in a thoughtful and caring manner.

Tranquility and Silence

Tranquility should be included in the art of teaching. Helping students to screen out noise and giving them a moment of silence would enable them to get in touch with themselves. Cultivating tranquility can help students to reduce or control the roaring, conflicting messages constantly flashed at them through the mass media and the wider environment. Jammed by external voices, students have had little room to listen to their inner selves and develop insights about themselves and the world. Going within is essential for expanding vision and the ability to embrace others.

In teaching, teachers should urge students to place great importance on spiritual growth in life, as opposed to obsession with material possessions. While students are encouraged to use their minds to think, they are also inspired to use their intuition and imagination to explore and feel. Students are encouraged to set goals in life that enable them to serve people and to help make the world a better place. They learn that we can shrink our ego and enlarge our soul if we let go of attachments to material possessions and pleasures of the senses and create more room to reflect and meditate. Teaching methods should enhance students' sensitivity in their hearts and souls in order to examine the multiple forces guiding the functioning of our Mother Earth and the universe. Thus, tranquility is not only sitting still, rather, it is an active attitude of recovering the inner wisdom deeply embedded in us. Gandhi says,

> Silence is a great help to a seeker after truth like myself. In the attitude of silence, the soul finds the path in clearer light, and what is elusive and deceptive resolves itself into crystal clearness. Our life is a long arduous quest after truth, and the soul requires inward restfulness to attain its full height. (Gandhi 1999, p. 52)

Gandhi further says:

> Modern civilization has taught us to convert night into day and golden silence into brazen din and noise. What a great thing it would be if we in our busy lives, could retire into ourselves each day, for at least a couple of hours, and prepare our minds to listen to the voice of the great silence. The divine radio is always singing if we could only make ourselves ready to listen to it, but it is impossible to listen without silence. (Gandhi 1999, p. 81)

The silence here is the space in which the soul communicates with the heart and mind. Without silence we cannot hear our soul's voice. Students would learn to exercise "active" silence, to hear the hearts of all people and all existences. Silence in environment, and silence between classes, is urged, not for religious observation—although it would be helpful to have a deep belief but not a closed mind—but to tune up our senses and the whole of our bodies to feel the spirits of all people and existences, to feel the energy from all forms of life, to envision our location in the web of life that is all alive and interlocking in energy and spirit.

Learning Humility and Simplicity

Humility originates with knowing that we are only one element in the universe, that we can be who we are because of the love and care of many people and because of the generosity of Mother Nature. Humility comes from recognizing that we can learn something from all people and circumstances; it allows us to see that the universe is moral (Tutu 1999, pp. 86–87) and to notice the virtues in all existences. Humility opens to students a wide spectrum of opportunities to learn. For example, how have people of different cultures learned to survive in dire circumstances? What creative ways do animals invent to survive the cold winter? With a sense of humility, we also deeply respect those people who are less educated than we are, who have lower social status, are doing a lower-paid job, for we discover with our soul's eyes we are all born with our own uniqueness. Humility lowers us to the position of a receiver, and we become uplifted by being able to absorb wisdom and support from all people and existences as our teachers.

Education is a truth-finding process. How do we find truth? As Gandhi says,

> There is so much untruth being delivered in a bewildered world. All that I can, in true humility, present to you is that truth is not to be found by anybody who has not got an abundant sense of humility. If you would swim on the bosom of the ocean of truth, you must reduce yourself to zero. (Gandhi 1999, p. 51)

Compassion, humility, and simplicity are three treasure-like virtues we need to possess, as Lao Zi instructs in his 5,000-word classic *Dao De Jing*. Thus, having compassion for all, lowering our egos, and giving the benefits of our actions to others while demanding very little for ourselves are inseparable virtues. Compassion empowers us, humility expands us (like the virtue of water to be willing to stay in low places and in the process expands to become a sea and an ocean), and simplicity frees us. Simplicity takes away many attachments that disturb the mind and the heart. Once we are able to do this, we can concentrate on serving and giving. What really matters is our contribution to the world. Taking a new perspective on life is the key to happiness. We need to urge our students to enrich their lives by going within to search for joy rather than going outside to rely on material things to fill up the void in their souls. Compassion, simplicity, and humility are powerful ways to open ourselves to wise teaching and to nurture a sense of gratitude for life.

Sensitivity

Education should teach children to feel for others as vivid, living, breathing human beings. We should engage students in the constant search of the heart, feeling the pain of suffering, the joy of giving, the serenity of an all-encompassing compassion, and the beauty of harmony. The heart that senses, feels, touches, is touched. Through learning with the heart, we develop a higher level of sensitivity. This sensitivity is critical for fostering attributes of compassion, sympathy, and concern for social justice and equality.

Direct Contact with Nature

In the school for love, the distance between school and nature is shortened. Nature is treated as a big classroom for students to learn about the wonder of the universe and life. Students learn about nature through activities such as learning to name animals, birds, and plants, and connecting the names with their vivid personalities and virtues. We need to render nature as alive and real to students. Students are encouraged to see all species in nature as friends and residents of the Earth community. They learn to feel the pain and sorrow of all natural existences as well. Thus, when we hear about environmental disasters, instead of reacting with indifference, students explore ways the environment can be improved to avoid future disasters. Being environmentally conscious, teachers open classroom windows to let fresh air in, open school doors to let in the singing of the birds, and let students out to touch and feel what is happening outside the classroom with every change of season.

Direct Contact with People around the World

A powerfully effective way of breaking down the wall of stereotypes and prejudices is to make direct contact with people. This kind of contact puts a face to the name, enabling students to see all people as concrete beings, rather than statistical numbers or abstract terms. Overseas studies, helping students to travel to "strange" places, should be a very important part of education. Twenty-first-century education will be truly international, globalized education. As national borders and cultural barriers are broken down, learning with people from around the world, with people literally sitting together or talking to each other daily (Internet technology has made this possible) will be the reality.

A documentary called "Promise" (2001) portrayed how several Palestinian and Israeli children were raised in a violent environment where hatred and a mentality of revenge were reinforced daily. But direct contact made the children realize that they are all human beings, and that violence is a losing game, and both sides suffer. In playing together, eating food, learning to dance, playing with balls together, friendship was built quickly, and love emerged.

Globally, we need to start cultural dialogues through children. Getting to know each other as equal, authentic human beings from an early age is paramount to building a peaceful and loving world. Sending students to study and make friends abroad is much more effective at deterring wars than building cross-continental weapons of defense.

Caring Integrated throughout the Process of Education

Caring means the ability to reach out to all students with sensitivity and authentic concern. It means that students are not depositories but vivid human beings who thrive on the nutrition of love and respect. Caring entails treating students as whole beings, and interaction is based on respect and concern from the heart.

Creativity and Imagination

Love is an incredibly creative energy. With love, we extend our interest and concern to all human affairs, to the whole natural environment and the universe. We stretch ourselves to the remotest places and delve deeply into the atoms of a flower. We become cocreators of life when we emulate love and live love in all moments of our life. Love enables us to break free from a narrow self-image and imagine a new world and a new universe with a profound beauty and harmony. Love is the most creative force that can give our imaginations great power. With love, our students will use their imaginations for a loving and caring world, for a reality where no children in the future will have to suffer the pain of war and conflict, where all species will have their rightful place.

SCHOOL CURRICULUM

Curriculum in the school for love requires a significant restructuring. For example, in language, we teach students the power of language, that whatever we say has a direct impact on our own and others' lives. We teach students to use positive language to encourage each other and find common ground; we use stimulating literary work that enhances students' desire to love and care. In history, we reveal to students how hatred has brought tremendous suffering to humanity as a whole, that both victims and victimizers have suffered. For example, the victimizers suffer the wasting of opportunities to experience and create love in the world, and the victims suffer the pain of disrespect and humiliation. In science, we teach students the power and limitations of science. We remind students of the critical importance of the integrated development of body, mind, and spirit. In this, we include marginalized subject areas in science and social science classes, including human emotions, human morality, and human spirituality. Children are taught that the universe is a living, conscious system and organism, and that our every act has an impact on its well-being. In all subjects, students learn that we are all divine souls, and that love is hope, love is energy, love is joy, and that we are a positive force in building a better world.

Based on these strategies, our school curriculum teaches students about world poverty, social injustices, violence in our life and in the world. Not only are these topics of discussion, but also students are urged to put their hearts out to feel the suffering in the world caused by these problems.

SCHOOL CULTURE

The culture permeating the school for love is one of harmony. When there is suffering from a loss in the family, willing hands will be there to help wipe away the tears; whoever has a disturbing question in the heart, safety is provided for the child to open up and carry on a dialogue in a supportive environment. People who have made mistakes are not looked down upon; rather, sincere support, understanding, and forgiveness are offered, along with a holistic analysis of the causes leading to the acts. Students are immersed in the air of love; wherever they go, they breathe it in and feel it. Teachers and students are engaged in constant discussion of the meaning events in daily life present to them, to help them understand gives them love and joy.

In the school for love, there is the earnest yearning for enlightenment, for moral and spiritual growth. Virtues such as love, care, respect, forgiveness, and understanding are taught and discussed without apology. They are treated as important skills and abilities for people to live meaningful and successful lives. A harmonious atmosphere encourages students to bring out differences in their beliefs and customs, but more importantly, it empowers them to build common ground. There will be no threats for voicing different opinions. The safe environment enables students and teachers to see the wonder and values of different cultures.

LEARNING IN DAILY LIFE

Schools for love will provide students the daily experience of working cooperatively, giving and receiving love, forgiving and understanding each other, and building bridges of understanding. The goal of school for love is that students form strong values and habits as loving people who are given an abundance of opportunities to experience the joy and power of love.

School for love is not difficult to implement if we urge ourselves and our students to start every day with a kind thought, to say a kind word, and to do a good deed whenever possible. Even when we are facing challenging moments, we can take this as a great opportunity to transcend ourselves and learn a greater form of love. If we have been wronged, it is a good opportunity to learn forgiveness; if a person is in need, it is a good opportunity to learn giving; if a person is sick, it is a chance to learn caring. For those people who have made big mistakes, even greater resolve to love and forgive is needed to understand the causes of their deeds based on the experiences of their lives and to know that we could have helped these individuals all along. In all, the overall culture is to seek transformation rather than condemnation, to aspire to higher realization of the grand beauty of life through the exercise of unconditional love rather than to diminish each other.

REDEFINING SUCCESS AND EXCELLENCE

"Success" in today's definition is based on a few factors: (1) wealth, (2) power, (3) education, (4) income, and (5) status. Very few definitions focus on a person's internal qualities: the capacity to love, the capacity to be forgiving and helpful, and wisdom. Because of the materialistic notion of success, schools focus on external indicators that are "important" for the students' future, such as grades, titles, money, and so on.

In the school for love, success and excellence are more internal than external. Students study to cultivate the attributes that make them loving, caring, forgiving beings. Success is reciprocal. Excellence is not being more competitive in exams, defeating other people, but rather nurturing a sense of true equality among all people and the appreciation of true beauty among all existences. It is knowing what really lasts—love that gives meaning to life, that extends joy and happiness to all.

Thus, school goals, curriculum, and teacher-student relationships should be transformed to make learning to love and care the central theme of education. Success and excellence are to be perceived in this framework.

AFFIRMING CHILDREN'S PROPENSITIES
AND GOOD NATURE

The school for love consistently affirms children's good nature and propensities to love, care, respect, and connect with all beings and creations in the universe. Children know a lot more than we think. They know what is right and what is wrong. They have a very keen sense of whether people are lying or not. They express a genuine love to all people and the natural world. They do not differentiate between the richer and the poorer, this race and that race—they accept unconditionally who we are. They have an especially sensitive heart for nature. They express great joy seeing animals and have the ability to blend themselves into the beauty of a flower. They have incredible imaginations. In their minds, they create constantly. They have a high spiritual sense—they believe in angels, in legends, in fantasies. If we refrain from our condescending "adults are all-knowing" view and take a new look at these qualities, we see children's genuine ability to love, to embrace! These are powers that can mold a new world! If we start their education by reinforcing those traits, and learn from children's ability to love unconditionally, then we may want to seriously consider: Are we teaching the children, or are the children teaching us?

Children are innocent, pure, and honest; children are serene, for they are not bound by excessive desires; they are open and sincere; they are intuitive and kind. We should treat these qualities in children like the most precious goods in the world. Their knowing is the most direct. The school for love urges children to keep and guard these qualities, to be deeply appreciative of their direct connections with the living world, with the living souls and hearts of people. We encourage them to see animals, flowers, clouds, people of all countries as equal, as living and spiritual beings. It is in these qualities that children have the greatest potential to become workers of love and creativity. Our current education tends to kill children's innocence and curiosity in the process of schooling. We need a major shift in focus in education so we can make a new start.

TEACHERS

In the school for love, school is conceived to be the site to empower students with habits and skills for learning to love in their lives. Teachers are therefore teachers of souls. They are role models who harbor unconditional love and compassion for all their students. Today, teachers are under a multitude of external pressures. Often they have to teach for tests and teach for salary. It is true that many teachers derive a great deal of joy from their teaching careers, and most are teaching from their hearts and souls. But today many find they do not have time to shower students with love, creating living experiences that teach students that love is a central value in life.

In the school for love, teachers see their role in a new perspective: They are building a new world that will be peaceful and loving. The children they teach will be global citizens who will accept no other means except love and peace as the ways to resolve our problems. The teachers are peace workers. To do this requires that teachers adopt the belief that only love can transform us internally, and internal changes will effect external changes. Thus, they aspire to fill the children's little hearts with big love; they teach children the values of forgiving others and being forgiven; they teach children the reciprocal benefits of being loving, kind, understanding, forgiving, respectful people. They teach children to see beauty in all existences. They teach children about the power they have if they base their thoughts, speech, and deeds on the foundation of love. They see the meaning of their work in expanding love, glorifying love, sharing love. They aim to work with a vision, one that will bring true changes to society. They see that human and environmental survival and prosperity are connected to their day-to-day work in the classroom.

Teachers are workers of the heart and the soul. Having undergone dramatic transformation of their own awareness, they are able to embrace all students with love, to see nature and the whole universe with a loving eye. They know the true meaning of life's purpose, and they have an expanded and long-term view of the ability and mission of education. They treat their work as sacred work. Teachers do not only teach. They are also active learners. They learn from parents, colleagues, and their students. For them, life is first a pursuit of love before they can teach love.

SCHOOL ADMINISTRATORS

School administrators have important roles to play in the school for love. They are the facilitators and active workers of love. In their position, they have the opportunity to demonstrate love through service, love through respect and understanding. They know what loves entails for our world. They have a deep understanding of the power of love. School administrators have a vital role in creating a culture of love in the school. They work to bring school goals, curriculum, teaching, and learning into a natural, synchronistic performance of learning to love. They treat students as budding flowers that can blossom into the wonder of a garden; they see teachers as their gardeners. Administrators perform their role in terms of service rather than as wielders of power.

ON HIGHER EDUCATION

In higher education, the norm has been to teach students to think with their minds, but little emphasis is placed on helping them to feel with their hearts and explore with their souls. We have become apathetic toward many urgent social issues while we claim to exercise our "reasoning" power. We criticize all kinds of social evils, at the individual and structural level, while we often fail to ponder constructive, transformative measures for making changes; thus, we generate more frustration than we solve problems. As highly vocal intellectuals, we grossly underutilize our powerful voice—the voice of love and conscience—to promote a better society and a kinder world. We become compartmentalized and pigeonholed in our academic fields and limit ourselves to give just a "rational" voice, to appear "scholarly" or "professional." We therefore disempower ourselves and fail to think and act for the good of all humanity. There needs to be a big turnaround in the philosophy and practice of higher education.

In social science and education, teachers in university classrooms ask students to be critical, and while a lot of frustration has been aroused, few solutions been found. To a great extent, this is not "spiritually" helpful—for spirituality works best in the atmosphere of harmony. The hope for us to achieve an awakening to social injustices is through using our hearts and souls to feel the pain of disadvantaged people, not only through using objective "theories" or rhetoric.

We should not be bound by too many theories to the point that we have lost our authentic selves, our creativity and imagination. Too often, we have allowed objectivity to conceal our own conscience and separated what we teach from what we believe in. We should teach students knowledge; more importantly, we should teach students to transcend knowledge and elevate their world views and open their hearts to a higher level of understanding. We should not play too much with academic terminologies; rather, we should encourage frank and direct expression of our thoughts.

A critically important task in higher education is the cultivation of a great heart that cares for the well-being of our world, our Earth. Students should develop an earnest desire to seek wisdom and enlightenment.

CONCLUSION

The role of education needs a dramatic shift: The priority of education should be to create loving, caring, and sensitive human beings. Children become loving beings in the environment of family, community, school, and the larger society. They learn what it means to be loving and to be loved. They bring sunshine wherever they go—they are beings highly capable of being compassionate, loving, respectful, forgiving, and tolerant.

School for love is a place that gives students the opportunity to be themselves —their genuine selves, each being a precious person. They have the skills to solve daily problems, based on a higher understanding of human life. The school helps young students to develop wisdom, to view life from a holistic, spiritual perspective. In the school for love, "knowing is loving," as Palmer (1993) eloquently states:

> The goal of a knowledge arising from love is the reunification and reconstruction of broken selves and worlds. A knowledge born of compassion aims not at exploiting and manipulating creation but at reconciling the world to itself. The mind motivated by compassion reaches out to know as the heart reaches out to love. Here, the act of knowing *is* the act of love, the act of entering and embracing the reality of the other, of allowing the other to enter and embrace our own. In such knowing we know and are known as members of one community, and our knowing becomes a way of reweaving that community's bonds.
>
> The origin of knowledge *is* love. (p. 8)

By choosing to build our schools for love, we are not leaving our future to chance; rather, we are building our future for hope. Palmer (1993) goes on to say,

> A knowledge that springs from love will implicate us in the web of life; it will wrap the knower and the known in compassion, in a bond of awesome responsibility as well as transforming joy; it will call us to involvement, mutuality, accountability. (p. 9)

Chapter Four

The Development of Integrated Intelligence: Intellectual, Emotional, Moral, Spiritual, and Ecological Intelligences

What is intelligence? Is intelligence mainly the function of the brain? As a whole person, can education in the 21st century ignore the fact that we are also emotional, moral, spiritual, and ecological beings? In the face of the tremendous challenges and crises we are living with, what kind of global citizens do we want to educate?

In the 20th century, intelligence has been narrowly defined as the capacity for abstract thinking, and verbal, written, and mathematical skills. Education ignores the notion that we use not only our minds to think, but also our hearts to feel and our souls to experience the meaning of life, and that all individuals are multifaceted beings. Separation of church and state has resulted in the relegation of our spiritual pursuits to the private realm, and fear of allegations of preaching certain doctrines forces teachers to marginalize education about spiritual and moral virtues. As Palmer (1998) critically points out,

The world of education as we know it is filled with broken paradoxes—and with the lifeless results:

- We separate head from heart. Results: minds that do not know how to feel and hearts that do not know how to think.
- We separate facts from feelings. Results: bloodless facts that make the world distant and remote and ignorant emotions that reduce truth to how one feels today.
- We separate theory from practice. Results: theories that have little to do with life and practice that is uninformed by understanding.
- We separate teaching from learning. Results: teachers who talk but do not listen and students who listen but do not talk. (p. 66)

41

Furthermore, we have allowed the narrow interests of the capitalist economy to define what education is for, employing rigid and limiting criteria to measure students, which is a detriment to their full creative potential, making most of them feel that they are failures.

Howard Gardner (1993) has expanded our view of intelligences by putting forward a multiple intelligence theory. He posits that we have at least eight intelligences. They are linguistic intelligence ("word smart"); logical-mathematic intelligence ("number/reasoning smart"); spatial intelligence ("picture smart"); bodily-kinesthetic intelligence ("body smart"); musical intelligence ("music smart"); interpersonal intelligence ("people smart"); intrapersonal intelligence ("self smart"), and naturalistic intelligence ("nature smart").

By the latter part of the 20th century, the idea of the existence of emotional intelligence attracted much attention as it speaks to many people's hearts. Goleman (1995) posits that IQ at best contributes about 20 percent to the factors that determine life success, which leaves 80 percent to other forces (p. 34). Indeed, educators and parents alike have found that ignoring the development of students' emotional abilities has resulted in neglect of students' emotional needs and distortion of children's personalities. The theory enables many to see that the development of children's abilities to handle human relations and control themselves is as important as IQ for success in life.

Are there other kinds of intelligences? Gardner (1999) and others (Borba 2001; Coles 1997) in recent years have speculated on the existence of moral and spiritual intelligence, yet this perspective is not included in serious scholarly and public discourse where it is still treated as a "subjective" area with insufficient scientific evidence.

If we accept that love is at the core of our essence, and that we are interconnected with all other beings and existences, we notice that virtues form the foundation of the universe's harmonious working (Yan Xin, 1996c). Based on this perspective, we must point not only to our brains but also to our hearts and souls for abilities to learn. We cannot limit our abilities to our intellect and sacrifice the other qualities we know we have, which are equally if not more important for our life's success and fulfillment. Our intelligences should reflect *our holistic ability* to live a meaningful life characterized by love, care, interconnectedness, and giving.

When we harbor deep love for all people and for all existences, we start to see a child as a whole person. We start to realize that each and every child is a wonder, and that the universe is a mystery; all people and existences are beautiful in their own right, and people's similarities are far greater than their differences. We start to see the diverse interests and potentials in students as powerfully exciting, mutually complementing and enriching, rather than as abnormal or problematic. We want our children to grow up intellectually, emotionally, morally, spiritually, and ecologically. We want children to have a high intellect, along with a loving, compassionate heart and an enlightened soul. We therefore need to facilitate the integrated development of students' IQ, EQ (emotional intelligence), MQ (moral intelligence), SQ (spiritual intelligence), and EcoQ (ecological intelligence). The integrated development of students' intelligences is a necessary condition for raising educated people and responsible global citizens.

To cultivate students' integrated intelligence necessitates the expansion of the horizon of teaching methods, and one key requirement is for teachers to creatively incorporate ways to enrich and expand students' inner hearts and heighten their sensitivity to feel and experience for all people and existences. Schools need to work on the "soft" or "intangible" areas that have been ignored in education, and to review traditional and modern teaching methods that enable students to cultivate their intelligences as integrated people. Teaching whole people and cultivating students' multifaceted intelligences can benefit both students and teachers.

DEFINITIONS AND IMPORTANCE FOR AN INTEGRATED PERSPECTIVE ON INTELLIGENCE

IQ is traditionally defined as the ability to analyze, synthesize ideas, and recall information. It tests a student's verbal ability—the accumulation of a large vocabulary, and—more importantly—the understanding of these words. It tests a person's spatial ability—the ability to manipulate objects in the mind (primarily by visual means); for example, rotating a three-dimensional object to see if it matches another object. It examines a person's visual ability—often associated strongly with the spatial tasks, it is the ability to visualize things, to compare pictures to their real-life counterparts, to complete pictures, and so on. It tests a person's pattern recognition—the ability to realize abstract patterns—and allows a person to apply these patterns from one problem to another. And, finally, memory is a vital element in IQ. This is the ability to hold data in mind while working on other parts of a problem.

EQ has been defined as the ability to "motivate oneself and persist in the face of frustration; to control impulse and delay gratification; to regulate one's moods and keep distress from swamping the ability to think; to emphasize and to hope (Goleman 1995, p. 34). It includes the dimension of self-awareness, in the sense of recognizing feelings and building a "vocabulary" for them; it pertains to managing one's emotions, respecting differences, and learning the arts of cooperation, conflict resolution, and negotiating compromise (p. 268).

IQ and EQ have achieved wide recognition today. However, moral intelligence is only beginning to be discussed (Borba 2001; Coles 1997). In schools today, the attributes of virtue are considered subjective choices rather than capacities and abilities inherent in us and necessary for our success in life. Yet in all major world religions, moral abilities are stressed above our other abilities. In Eastern philosophy and religions, such as Confucianism, Taoism, and Buddhism, moral abilities are fundamental for one's success in life. Anyone seeking success must start with cultivating virtues, as demonstrated by benevolence, compassion, respect, humility, equality, forgiveness, and responsibility. They are deemed primary conditions for a harmonious society, and for individuals, they free the brain of chaotic thoughts, bring clarity to the mind, and reveal the wisdom deep within us. From a Taoist perspective (Lin 2005), virtues are the manifestation of the great Tao in human society. The ultimate goal is a full, deep understanding of the working of the universe and the ability to act in tandem with the Tao, or the Way.

In Western philosophy, Plato teaches that knowledge must be connected with virtues in order for one to have wisdom. In Christianity, loving people is the pathway to God, the ultimate truth. Having moral virtues is a conscious choice for one to be in line with the higher force of the universe.

Michele Borba, in her book *Building Moral Intelligence* (2001), defines character as moral intelligence in terms of seven core virtues: empathy, conscience, self-control, respect, kindness, tolerance, and fairness. She states,

> Moral intelligence is the capacity to understand right from wrong; it means to have strong ethical convictions and to act on them so that one behaves in the right and honorable way. This wonderful aptitude encompasses such essential life characteristics as the ability to recognize someone's pain and to stop oneself from acting on cruel intentions; to control one's impulse and delay gratification; to listen openly to all sides before judging; to accept and appreciate differences; to decipher unethical choices; to empathize; to stand up against injustices; and to treat others with compassion and respect. (p. 4)

Borba believes these are the core traits that will help children become decent, good human beings; they are the bedrock of solid character and strong citizenship. She places empathy in the forefront of the seven virtues. While I agree with her, I think without the cultivation of universal and unconditional love for all beings as our equals, we have no solid foundation for empathy and all the other virtues to stand on; we cannot hope for children to act out the virtues she outlines. Having a strong sense of interconnectedness and oneness is critical if we wish to treat others as we treat ourselves.

In this book, MQ is defined as the ability to act, speak, and think in accordance with the virtues of love, compassion, care, understanding, forgiveness, and responsibility. The student knows what is right and wrong, and treats all people and all existences with a sense of equality and kindness. MQ is the ability to reciprocate, to integrate one's speech and acts along the line of the common good.

Gardner (1999) muses on spiritual intelligence, but he is not definite about it. In the past few years, more people are beginning to accept spirituality as a form of intelligence. Here, SQ is defined as the ability to understand the higher meaning of life, and the ability to connect with people and existences at the spiritual level. It is the ability to cut through superficial differences and see divinity in all souls. SQ enables us to find meaning and purpose in what we do, and look deep into ourselves to see who we are, and to connect with the spirits of all people and all creations in the universe. It emphasizes the development of wisdom, a deep knowing of the purpose of life from a holistic perspective.

Ecological intelligence has not been developed fully in our current education training programs. In Eastern philosophy, however, especially Chinese philosophy, which sees that human beings can achieve complete harmony with nature, and in Buddhism, which treats all existences as a linked web with a vital need for mutual respect, ecological intelligence is a given. In this book, I argue that EcoQ exists as sensitivity toward everything in nature and in the universe. It is the ability to feel and experience the interconnectedness of all lives and all forms of existences. It is a deep sense of compassion and connection, a oneness that is intuitively experienced. EcoQ is an innate ability of young children, as demonstrated by their ability to connect with and understand animals, plants, and all that is in nature.

Why is the integrated development of students' IQ, EQ, MQ, and SQ important? A study of our world traditions and religions reveals that most of their teachings and practices emphasize the nurturing of the body, mind, and spirit as an integrated system. Love, compassion, respect, interconnectedness, forgiveness, sensitivity—all these are seen as attributes as well as abilities to be cultivated in a fulfilled life. Love, compassion, forgiveness, humility, and respect form a common thread linking the world's greatest traditions and works. We as educators are challenged to draw from ancient wisdom and venture into new frontiers with courage to explore effective ways to transform future global citizens holistically. Teaching for the development of students' integrated intelligences means the teacher-student relationship is based on trust and mutual exploration of the meaning of life. Hierarchy must be broken down, and children's ability to connect with people and all existences must be seen as they having as much to teach adults as adults have to teach them. Students should be empowered to see that their purpose is to lead wisdom-guided lives, enhancing life's values through working for others and the universe, while at the same time bringing themselves to a higher level of spiritual enlightenment.

A NEW PERSPECTIVE ON IQ DEVELOPMENT

Challenging the Current Notion of IQ

To a large extent, we are living in the myth of disconnections. Our schools pretend that students can be whole while focusing only on their intellectual development. IQ has been pitched as the ultimate concern of education and made the measure of a student's worth. We emphasize this so much that we relegate the development of students' emotional, moral, and spiritual intelligences to the business of the private domain, ignoring the development of these many capacities in students.

This neglect has come with a dire consequence. Our schools have turned out people who have very high IQs but who are capable of killing their fellow human beings without any sense of guilt. These people—scientists, politicians, professionals, military personnel—develop their high IQs without learning to love or developing a profound understanding of human oneness. Hence, a new kind of IQ is needed, one that must be undergirded by love, compassion, and responsibility. Educators responsible for our future necessarily see that high IQ is to be linked with high EQ, MQ, EQ, EcoQ, and SQ, and that our intelligence is *not* independent of our moral, emotional, and spiritual cultivation. An individual will not be considered to have a high IQ who does not have the ability to love, to know what is right and wrong. It is high time to bring the notion of love and care into the discussion of IQ.

New Pathways to IQ Development?

One belief from traditional wisdom in Chinese culture is that reciprocal love in a family is crucial for IQ development. Discoveries in life science indicate that we inherit our DNA and RNA from our parents. Could it be that knowledge accumulated by generations of our ancestors is embedded in the coding system? If disease can be passed on, can knowledge and wisdom also be passed on? Is there a key to inheriting and unearthing knowledge that has been created and stored up in our biological system?

In Confucian, Taoist, and Buddhist cultures, as well as in the original teachings of Christianity and Islam, respect for one's parents, for elderly people, and for our teachers is not taken as a choice but is stressed as essential. In fact, in many cultures, perennial wisdom is that children need to be respectful of the elderly to be successful in life. Respect for all people, and especially respect for the elderly, is considered one of the highest virtues. In Chinese Taoist concepts of longevity and immortality, it is believed that our ancestors stored boundless energy and wisdom; and in Buddhism, respect for one's parents and for all people is treated as the key to becoming enlightened. In Confucianism, filial piety is not only a kind of social morality, it is also a "heavenly virtue." Mystics teach us that such a virtue contains the key to opening wisdom and tapping into the energy stored up by past generations.

Filial piety in Eastern philosophy entails children loving their parents, who give them life and bring them up with unconditional love. Pious children take the advice of parents, striving to fulfill their expectations, caring about and supporting their parents, burying them and memorializing them. Filial piety is seen as a heavenly virtue as it is first and foremost a natural response of children to reciprocate their life givers' love. It is through this reciprocity that we inherit intelligence from our ancestors.

Loving one's parents is the starting point for loving others. Eastern culture believes that if one cannot love one's own parents, then one cannot be expected to love others. With love for our own parents, we have the grounding to love the parents of others and, further, all people on Earth. According to the *Book of Filial Piety*, "those who love their family members do not dare to harm others; those who respect their family members do not dare to neglect others." So it is said, "filial piety and love for siblings are connected with divinity; they develop between heaven and earth and embody everything." Loving our own family and others is thus a mechanism to open up our ability to learn. There is no separation of our intellectual development and our knowing how to love and respect.

In Taoist culture, a sage must be highly respectful of all elderly people as their own parents, and this is treated as a necessary technique for unlocking the energy and the knowledge stored up by generations of people. Hence, piety is not only treated as a social virtue, it is also a functional mechanism for enlightenment. Greatly influenced by Taoism and Confucianism, Chinese educational tradition has long emphasized respect for one's parents and for those older than us. Strongly built into the culture is a belief that one cannot expect to be successful, and one cannot avoid making mistakes in life, if one does not listen to the wisdom of those who have treaded the path and accumulated a lot of knowledge and experience. Confucianism helps institutionalize this virtue by setting up a social structure where parents are obligated to give their love and care to their children, and children in return are respectful and loving.

In today's society, the teaching of piety is greatly downplayed in our education. Should we begin to study the reciprocal love in family, and reciprocal love from one to another, as a key to stored up knowledge and wisdom by generations of people? Developments in life science may eventually point to a biological and physiological basis for this. The ideology of individualism posits individuals as independent entities responsible ultimately for their own well-being. Yet according to science, we cannot learn without the passing of the genetic code from our parents. We must bring the understanding of reciprocity of love and care into the understanding of intelligence.

EQ DEVELOPMENT

Likewise, love, respect, forgiveness, and repentance create reciprocal social relationships in society. Howard Gardner, in his description of multiple intelligences, lists interpersonal and intrapersonal relationships as part of human intelligence. It is Daniel Goleman (1995), however, who brings the concept of emotional intelligence to the forefront of educators' attention. Developing students' emotional intelligence has multiple benefits for them; for example, it helps them understand what causes feelings; it develops their skills for expressing anger; it encourages them to exhibit more positive feelings about themselves, school, and family; it teaches them how to handle stress better; it helps them accept another person's perspective; it increases their ability to understand relationships, and so on (pp. 283–284).

However, Goleman and others discuss the role of EQ at a narrow, individualistic level. I believe that for true development of EQ, it must be linked to our essence as loving souls—that is, we must be loving, caring, respectful, and forgiving in order to develop our emotional intelligence. We need to consciously cultivate love and compassion before we can be emotionally intelligent. The ability to empathize with others, to take the stand of others and understanding our own and others' emotions, to cooperate, and to be tolerant all need to come from deep-seated love and understanding. Relationship is mutual; it is in giving and being respectful that we receive love and are respected. Hence, development of emotional intelligence needs to expand to a wider circle of social concern for the good of others as well as oneself.

In the world we are living in, we feel great pressures and helplessness in our lives. The marginalization of emotional intelligence and the disintegration of communities have created hosts of crises in people's lives. We need to see our work and lives as reciprocal with those of others, slow down our pace, and listen to the inner voice enabling the communication of our minds with our souls. When we cultivate diverse levels of tranquility, our subconsciousness is freed from the restraints of daily life, and we can see the connections of all human beings and things with enhanced clarity of mind and stability of emotions, and a much clearer picture about the purpose of life emerges.

To foster students' EQ development, we need to "create a school climate characterized by a close, trusting relationship among students and between students and adults," and there is a "commitment to personalization and to engaging students and teachers in a familylike atmosphere" (Sergiovanni 1992, p. 114). The intimate feeling of others as oneself effectively reduces or takes away the feeling of separation, giving one a feeling of being wrapped in love and acceptance.

THE DEVELOPMENT OF MORAL INTELLIGENCE

Moral education has been viewed with doubt and often equated with religious preaching. Moral education has been relegated to the private domain for which families and church are mainly responsible. Teachers focus primarily on teaching students to comply with rules and shy away from touching on the fundamental values behind the rules. Why do we need to love and respect each other? Why do we have to be sensitive to others' feelings? These are often not discussed with children. The great void left in the development of students' morality has led to serious problems in education. A large number of people grow up not knowing what is right and what is wrong and have little respect and compassion for others. One example is reflected in apathy, when people look at sufferings of people dispassionately, as they are perceived to happen to "others," or they are "natural happenings."

To live morally requires moral intelligence. Moral choices are made not only in the brain, but also in the heart. Our conventional discussion of moral education has focused on the brain making choices, yet a truly moral person is a person who not only thinks but also feels and reaches out. Chinese philosophy states, "The hearts guide the souls of the divine." The philosophy of Chinese medicine posits that "the heart is the master of the whole being." Mystical Eastern beliefs also indicate that we have multiple existences in ourselves. We embody all that exists in the universe, and "the heart is the house of divine spirits." The location of moral intelligence may hence be in both the mind and the heart. It cannot be understood only from a psychological cognitive perspective.

Moral intelligence is connected with the development of IQ, EQ, and other intelligences. To use a metaphor, our moral abilities are the foundational pillar holding up other kinds of intelligence. Like other subject areas or fields of study, moral intelligence comprises attributes, capabilities that must be learned and mastered to navigate the boat of life for individuals and for a society. Scientific laws may be discovered in the 21st century that measure how our moral behaviors affect us physiologically. New theories may be advanced to explain the intricate relation of give and take, energy generation and diffusion, cause and effect, and so on.

The world we are living in is highly individualistic. Yet, we cannot be morally intelligent without working for the common good. In giving love, we harvest love and trust, and by helping and forgiving others we help ourselves to realize a state of freedom. Cultivating virtuous minds, hearts, and deeds, and building a balanced view of the relationship of give and take, will create new space in our hearts to embrace others and ourselves.

Living the principle of virtue in our daily lives can affect our biological and physiological systems in a positive manner. Reduction of anger and greed leads to a relaxation of our organs and our muscles and hence an improvement of our health. From a technical perspective, when we love, we receive support and trust in return; when we forgive, we free not only the others but mostly ourselves; when we repent, we allow ourselves to renew and re-create and leap to a higher level of growth. Virtues are embedded abilities in us, and we can choose to develop them.

We are living in the age in which making correct moral choices and decisions has become a survival issue. Globally, we are facing the threat of nuclear war and environmental breakdown due to pollution and excessive development. Socially we are living in a society beset by problems such as violence, drug abuse, and discrimination. Personally, we face the dilemma of having to judge right from wrong in complex situations, and to balance collective and individual interests. Furthermore, the information age creates "new frontiers for ethical considerations: artificial intelligence, cyberspace and virtual reality" (Kizza 1998, xiii). People can "surf" into any domain without much hindrance, which renders issues of moral judgment even more important. Moral intelligence becomes critical with the flooding of uncensored information, or even violent information available to the public.

We thus live in an era in which moral intelligence is critically needed so that we can differentiate what is right or wrong in an increasingly fragmented and complex society, and that so we can hold our moral stand in face of a multitude of influences.

Moral intelligence calls for shrinking the ego and enlarging the social consciousness for the common good. Our education should teach students to go beyond the notion that "I have the right to this and that," and instead ask, "What moral decisions should we make when we are facing a certain situation that would take into consideration the interests of all people?"

We can help our students learn meaningful lessons from both positive and negative events in life; we can point out to them the coexistence of opposing elements in life, enabling them to see that there is reason behind all that happens, that what is critical is to draw lessons and move on. For many negative happenings in the world, as well as for any positive happenings, we can reflect on whether we have played a part. All circumstances in which we find ourselves may present opportunities to understand life better, to transcend ourselves, and to learn the power of love. Overall, the development of moral intelligence calls for a transformation of epistemology and world outlook.

SPIRITUAL INTELLIGENCE

From the seventeenth century until the end of the 20th century, a scientific paradigm has dominated our life:

[This] approach secularized life, removing any vestige of the divine or the sacred from all things in existence. Its guiding metaphor was the machine. The universe was seen as one great clockwork mechanism, whose function could be predicted and controlled. In this era, explanations of life were sought in mechanical, linear, cause-and-effect processes, in empirical information gathered by the senses or by equipment serving to extend the senses' capabilities. (Nava 2001, p. 4)

Palmer also criticizes objectivism:

Modern knowledge has allowed us to manipulate the world but not to control its fate (to say nothing of our own), a fact that becomes more clear each day as the ecosystem dies and our human systems fail. Indeed, by disconnecting us from the world, objectivism has led us into actions so inharmonious with reality that catastrophe seems inevitable if we stay the course. Objectivism, far from telling the truth about how we know, is a myth meant to feed our fading fantasy of science, technology, power and control. (1998, p. 56)

Nava observes that success in technological development was accompanied by a profound dehumanization. "As a result, life lost its meaning, and the planet's natural resources were subjected to widespread depredation" (2001, p. 5). Nava holds that in contrast to reductionist, mechanistic understanding, we need a holistic vision in which the universe is a living network of relationships where "everything is interconnected, forming systems and subsystems. Human beings are one with this universe, and our consciousness is the consciousness of the universe" (p. 5). He further notes,

Spirituality is the realization that the individual is part of the whole; it is inherent beauty, truth, and all things unconditional. This experience brings about love, compassion, joy, humility, and interrelatedness. Spirituality is the creative energy of the universe. (p. 39)

In education, we have discussed the elimination of illiteracy and the elimination of functional illiteracy, yet we have seldom talked about the elimination of "spiritual illiteracy" (Walsch 1999, p. 21). Is there such a thing as spiritual intelligence?

We cannot live our lives without asking these questions at some point: Why do we live? Have we fulfilled our life's purpose? Are we being true to who we are? These questions indicate we are not mechanical beings but beings with souls who search for spiritual meaning in life. Although many people shuffle these questions to the back of their mind, there are moments when these questions come to their attention and force them to think and reflect. In the United States, more than half of the medical schools now offer courses such as spirituality and medicine, largely because patients are demanding more spiritual care at the end of their lives (Kalb 2003, p. 44).

What is spiritual intelligence? Emmons (1999), defining it from a psychological perspective, states that it is "the capacity to transcend the physical and material; the ability to experience heightened states of consciousness; the ability to sanctify everyday experiences; the ability to utilize spiritual resources to solve problems; and the capacity to be virtuous" (p. 164).

In this book, I define spiritual intelligence as the ability to be connected to the whole. It is the ability to transcend the restriction of the material and reach the higher realm of existence, the intuitive, spiritual, creative realm. Spiritual intelligence enables us to use our hearts and souls to speak with hearts and souls of all existences. It is the ability to experience unity in a seemingly separated world. Spiritual intelligence treats all human beings as equal souls that are perpetually engaged in the process of experiencing life, in search of love and higher knowing. Spiritual intelligence is connected with intuition:

> Intuition is more than just a spontaneous feeling; rather, it is the result of a spiritual growth which derives from long and penetrating preoccupation with a matter or a problem—leading to the identification of all the individual features of the object hitherto remained separate to specific reflection, and making them immediately present to the mind in all their connectedness. (Schonberger 1992, p. 18)

Spirituality is not religion, although religious practices can enhance one's spirituality. Spirituality is our ability to experience the whole; "it is an experience of wholeness, a total and direct experience of inner peace, love, and universal brotherhood, permitting the natural unfolding of human values (Nava 2001, p. 32).

Cultivating students' spiritual intelligence starts with the knowledge that children are innately good; they are by nature spiritual; they have full interest in exploring the meaning of life; and they know by nature what the "common good" is and what love entails. With this fundamental framework, we will nurture these qualities in children like a mother hen protecting her children;

we will look at our students with amazement and awe. We will marvel at their abilities; we will help them connect the self with their family, community, society, the world, and the universe. We will encourage them to share their experience of profound joy; we will appreciate their curious questions; we will understand how they feel when they describe the pain of animals being slaughtered rather than dismissing them.

Spiritual intelligence entails extending one's love from one's family to one's friends, neighbors, community, and all people in the world; to those people who have wronged us, and to those who have broken laws. For spiritual intelligence transcends the division of us and others. We are all one. Spiritual intelligence requires a higher perspective on life. Everything happens in the universe for a reason. While it is easy for us to love our families, loving strangers is one step further, and loving those people who have wronged us is a bigger step yet.

Spiritual intelligence also means holding conversations with all people and all existences. This conversation is carried out using our hearts to sense the joy and suffering of those around us; it is using our spirit to see all at the soul level. We see all happenings in an interconnected manner. We refrain from blaming and condemning, but evaluate and examine the full causes for certain behaviors and events. A sense of interdependence is created, with not only other people, "but all living creatures and the planet as a whole" (Nava 2001, p. 39).

Spiritual intelligence engages the deeper part of our brain and the whole of our being. Physiologically in Eastern mystical teaching, knowing resides in the frontal lobe where our "heaven eye" between the eyebrows can be opened, and also in our meridian points. Its development is rendered possible after we have given up hatred, after we create space for our spirit and soul to present its wisdom to us, after we start allowing the heart to feel. A supportive educational environment can bring an outpouring of revelations, wisdom, and incredible relief and joy. The development of spiritual intelligence is a healing process. All of these are connected with reducing our desires, creating spaces to hear our inner voice, meditating to reach deep into the true self. Development of spiritual intelligence is essentially an awakening process:

> Gradually, the heart begins to open, fear and anger melt, greed and jealousy dwindle, happiness and joy grow, love flowers, peace replaces agitation, concern for others blossoms, wisdom matures, and both psychological and physical health improve. Virtually all aspects of our lives are touched or transformed in some way. (Walsh 1999, p. 4)

Developing spiritual intelligence requires us to see all challenges in life in a different light. We need to ask these questions: What opportunities are presented in these challenges to transcend our personal biases and weaknesses? How do they help us to learn to love, care, forgive, respect, concentrate, and repent?

In our schools today, there is deep fear of bringing spirituality into education. We are afraid of being blamed for preaching religion, as "prejudice, fear, ignorance, and hatred, masquerading as religious belief, have powerfully shaped humankind's relationship to spirituality" (Noble 2001, p. 28); we are fearful of charges by parents and different social groups. It takes great courage to say that we must tend to our children's spiritual needs and that we cannot leave our children to grope in the dark. If spiritual growth touches on the core of our existence, pushing this out of education is irresponsible and harmful.

Spiritual education enhances the dimension and depth of students' lives and helps reveal to them who they are:

> There within ourselves, we finally find the most profound, the most meaningful, and the most important discovery any human being can make. Within ourselves we find our deepest self, our true self, and recognize that we are not only more than we imagined, but more than we can imagine. We see that we are a creation of the sacred, intimately and eternally linked to the sacred, and forever graced and embraced by the sacred.
>
> This is the greatest of all discoveries, the secret of all secrets, the priceless gift that is both the source and goal of the great religions. This is the aim of all our seeking, the answer to a life-time of longing, the cause of the mystic's bliss, the source of overwhelming and enduring joy. (Walsh 1999, p. 5)

When we open our doors to spiritual discussion, we allow students to ask questions such as, What is life for? How can we live life more meaningfully? How can we become more caring and compassionate? What attitudes should we adopt when we face challenges? How can we learn to love even though the circumstance seems to make it very difficult? How can we be more imaginative and creative? These questions need to be in our awareness daily, and moment to moment. With such keen awareness, we treat life and people not as abstract concepts but as vivid and sacred. We learn to broaden ourselves so that we can embrace and love just as the universe does. In submerging our purpose with that of all people and all existences, we fulfill our destiny. Spiritual intelligence hence pushes us to be larger than ourselves, and to be our true Self, which is interconnected with all people and existences. We consciously choose to be our larger Self rather than the self, through our words and deeds, creating who we are.

ECOLOGICAL INTELLIGENCE

Ecological intelligence is an innate ability of all species to live in harmony with their environment and to adjust to changes to be sustained and survive. A revealing example is Canadian geese seeking refuge from the fiercely cold weather in Canada by flying south every year. It is built into their system of intelligence. This is also true of the human species. For centuries, human beings have adjusted their lifestyles and moved to places where the environment suits them better. Our knowledge about the ecological system of the Earth and the universe is recorded in our DNA and RNA, which translates into habits and propensities that help us to survive in the natural environment.

In many cultures and religions, knowing nature is paramount. In Native American culture and religion, one is not separated from nature but lives as a part of nature. In the teachings of Buddhism and Hinduism, all existences come from the same source, and all have souls; hence, human beings are not separated from their surroundings. In Confucianism and Taoism, one can cultivate human-nature oneness in such a way that art works are injected with spirits of what they portray, be they mountains, rivers, flowers, animals, scenes, and so on. Nature is energy, it is spirit, it is alive and dynamic, and human beings are part of it. All existences can interpenetrate each other and become one with each other.

The American Indians believe that humans are threefold beings made up of spirit, mind, and body, and that plants and animals, like humans, are part of the spirit world. Of the three elements—spirit, mind, and body—the spirit is the most important. Education should aim at achieving harmony, that is, to be at oneness with life, eternity, the creator, and oneself (Reagan 2000, p. 86).

Taoists and Buddhists also believe that all existences are spirits, that they come from the same source as well. Compassion for all existences is the key concept in these two religions, fundamental in one's quest for enlightenment.

I conceptualize ecological intelligence as the ability to see life as an interconnected web. It is widely known that many animals have feelings and intelligence, and research reveals this is also true of plants (Tompkins and Bird 1989). Japanese Shintoists and indigenous groups around the world see mountains, the moon, and the sun all imbued with spirits and intelligence. An ecologically intelligent person connects with spirits of all existences.

What is fostered in the ecological intelligence is . . . the deep awareness of the sacred presence within each reality of the universe. There is an awe and reverence

due to the stars in the heavens, the sun, and all heavenly bodies; to the seas and
the continents; to all living forms of tress and flowers; to the myriad expressions
of life in the sea; to the animals of the forests and birds of the air. (Berry 1988,
p. 46)

With such intelligence, one sings the song of life with all existences, and
one acutely feels that "to wantonly destroy a living species is to silence forever a divine voice" (Berry 1988, p. 46). People with high ecological intelligence who have a genuine love for plants can cocreate with them. A person
with loving energy listens to the flowers and plants, and vice versa (Tompkins
and Bird 1989, p. 133).

We need to learn ecological intelligence from children, for they tend to see
plants and animals as alive, as friends, and know what they think and feel.
Hence, the development of ecological intelligence is not a top-down affair;
rather, it is adults learning from children and understanding how this intelligence can be maintained.

Ecological and spiritual intelligences are interconnected. They form a mutually enhancing relationship. A highly spiritual person necessarily has a
heightened sense of our ecological connectedness with all that exists in the
universe. A highly ecologically conscious person feels intensely the wholeness of people and natural existence, hence she or he is more able to connect
parts together and assume a holistic view of life and the universe. Future science may find that EcoQ can be located between our eyebrows in the
acupuncture points in our body, in the energy field of all existences.

INTEGRATING THE DEVELOPMENT OF
IQ, EQ, MQ, SQ, AND ECOQ

Our education should undergo a shift toward the development of the students'
integrated intelligence. Not only students' intellectual development is important; students also need to simultaneously develop abilities to be moral, spiritual, and ecological. They need smart minds as well as tender hearts; they
must know right from wrong; they must connect with all people and with
nature.

The age of only helping students with the acquisition of hardware, basic
facts, and formulas should be called to an end. We must treat the mastery of
intangibles such as values as essential in education. Children's emotional,
moral, spiritual, and ecological-awareness development are fundamental to
their becoming happy, responsible, whole people. The perspective of integrated holistic intelligence stresses the role of education in wisely training
students as global citizens, Earth residents, and citizens of the universe. Edu-

cation must expand its horizon, its vision, and its passion; educators must expand their hearts, minds, and souls to see far into the future. Only through this transformation can we save ourselves from destruction and move toward peace and harmony.

To conclude, we need a wholly new outlook on the universe, the world, and human society; a new epistemology; and new paradigms in science and social science to reconceptualize life, nature, and the universe. We need to undergo an expansion of theories such as psychoanalytic theory and learning theories. We need to take a serious look at virtue in education and its role in balancing our lives, emotions, and spiritual well-being. We need to pay attention to the role of piety in improving human IQ. We need to pay attention to our feelings and intuitions. Above all, we need to develop a vision which recognizes that our destiny and the hope for humanity depend on the gregarious nature and consciousness of all people in relation to themselves and to everything else in the universe.

Chapter Five

Education for Global Peace

What is the priority of education in the 21st century? As educators responsible for the training of future generations, in the face of the reality that the human race has amassed enough weapons to destroy all lives on Earth many times over, it is unavoidable that education in the 21st century must be education for global peace. Dr. Kings says,

> Somehow we must transform the dynamics of the world power struggle from the nuclear arms race, which no one can win, to a creative contest to harness man's genius for the purpose of making peace and prosperity a reality for all the nations of the world. In short, we must shift the arms race into a "peace race." (King 1964, p. 185)

For educators to pioneer a "peace race," a very far-reaching view must be adopted so that we clearly see where we set priorities. The offering of peace education cannot be sporadic efforts but systematic and synchronized efforts, involving all levels of education and all forces in society. We must lead our students to the crucial understanding of what and how horrible mistakes have been made, and what it takes for us to heal and reconstruct a new world through the power of love.

PRIORITIZING PEACE EDUCATION

Education as a powerful force for building a peaceful world calls for a thorough transformation of both educational theory and practice. The goals of education need to be shifted drastically from an emphasis on tests and efficiency to helping students build a love-based, care-based understanding of the world

and facilitating communication among human beings, and between humankind and nature.

Peace education in the 20th century was highly marginalized. Only a small
number of scholars and educators pay serious attention to peace education.
When it is studied, it is often subsumed in other forms of education such as
development education, international education, human rights education, and
so on (Harris and Morrison 2003). However, as we face the possibility of horrible destruction or even total annihilation, teaching our younger generation
to learn to live peacefully can no longer be shuffled aside, for only by fostering a great love and a respectful attitude for each other and only by embracing universal love can we transcend hatred. To survive, our children need to
know that arms races, war, and violent conflicts are no solution to any of our
problems, that these activities should be totally denounced, and that only an
all-encompassing love for each other can give us sustainable peace. Our education is ripe for expanding its vision—that is, rather than placing a narrow
emphasis on individualistic rights, we need to return to the nurturing nature
of human beings, emphasizing our ability to love reciprocally and
care responsibly for each other. An education that creates hope for a peaceful
future prioritizes the teaching of love, respect, forgiveness, and care for all
people.

Scholars have called for attention to peace education over the past few
decades. For example, teaching materials and teaching guides have been developed that integrate peace education into subjects in elementary and secondary schools (Harris and Morrison 2003; Smith and Carson 1998; Lantieri
and Patti 1996; Bey and Turner 1996; Lasley 1994; Hicks 1988; Reardon
1988). Unfortunately, this has not been reflected in the priorities of today's
educational research and policy. For example, government documents on education seldom mention the need for peace education at all, and few scholars
have made peace education their primary research focus and intellectual responsibility. Only one academic journal devoted to peace education exists,
and it was only launched in 2004. Only three graduate programs on peace education exist in the United States, and graduate courses on peace education
are few.

It is encouraging that more and more people are taking action and joining
the ranks. New courses are being created and offered; educators are springing
into action to create new curricula for peace education. Enlarging the ranks of
peace educators, however, requires more teachers and scholars that change
their stance from "objective observers" of global conflicts and the dangers of
war and become peace educators and advocates. Policy makers, researchers,
teachers, and community members need to work together as researchers and
advocates of peace education for a peaceful and loving world.

CHANGING OUR COLLECTIVE MINDSET FOR PEACE

Love is a peaceful consciousness. A collective change in mindset needs to take place before significant development in peace education takes place. When we begin to think collectively about peace education and bring others along, we take the first major step toward positive changes for peace in the world, because awareness precedes reality. Love is an emotion as well as positive energy, whereas anger and hatred are negative energy potentially creating danger to ourselves and the world. As David Bohm (1980) says, "Thought is material" (p. 53). Eastern philosophy and religion also instruct that our reality is a manifestation of our inner state of being. Hence, intention and acts of love by teachers will form the first wave of positive energy for changing the world for peace.

Thoughts and emotions are energies that affect physical realities. For example, when we are angry, our faces turn red and our hearts beat irregularly; when we are happy, our faces shine. Our reality has everything to do with what we think and say. Research has found that patients who are prayed for have better recoveries than those patients who are not prayed for (Dossey 1993). Thought-energy is sent out in the combined form of biological electrical magnetic waves, biological fields, and consciousness information. The speed of this kind of bio/electromagnetic/consciousness information energy is faster than the highest speed we know, which is light; thus, we have not been able to measure it with modern equipment. People with a high level of spiritual development and those with paranormal abilities can feel and see this field as matter, energy, bio-information, or thought form (Hunt 1996; Goodman 1979). The energy field from human thought can spread out and affect our social and physical environment, forming a kind of "bio-relativity" (Goodman 1979). In other words, our thoughts can affect changes in world happenings, including natural events such as rain or wind (Hunt 1996). American Indians have used dancing and chanting to communicate with nature, which is a way of tapping into the energy of nature. Now just imagine how powerful the energy of humanity's collective consciousness would be if six billion people residing on Earth simultaneously think about peace?

Based on this perspective, we can be transformed into peace educators at this moment by thinking about peace and wishing for peace. Our ideas of peace will send out vibrational signals to like-minded people and draw people of similar convictions together. We can begin to implement peace education by centering our awareness on peace-building virtues such as unconditional love, compassion, respect, and forgiveness for all people and all things in the world *by adjusting our mind right now.*

STARTING PEACE EDUCATION WITH YOUNG CHILDREN

Young children's thoughts are peaceful, as they are not yet contaminated by the many negative influences in their social environment. They have the ability to see others as themselves, as their brain (especially the forehead) carries a higher level of energy (Hunt 1996) that enables them to penetrate the collective unconscious of humankind and other existences, as they think nondifferentially. This is why religions and mystical teachings urge people to return to the state of a child, or a state of unity based on the energy of love. We are often so touched when we look into the eyes of young children, seeing purity, kindness, and joy, and we are sent to the sky by their hearty laughter. Children are by nature peaceful. Therefore, if our education allows children to be themselves, and if our schools help children maintain their peaceful propensities and consistently reinforce their peaceful consciousness throughout the process of education, there is hope of achieving everlasting peace and harmony on Earth.

All people have a "Buddhist seed" or "divine light" in their souls. This implies that we are born to be kind and loving people. Maria Montessori believes that all children have innate tendencies toward compassion and care for others, and education should establish an environment that allows the natural peace-loving instinct of children to flourish. As Harris and Morrison put it,

> Montessori believed that adults must become more like children if they are to achieve "heaven on earth." Children are trusting and open. Children have a love for others that provides the basis for peaceful coexistence on this planet. (2003, p. 48)

Hence, peace education is already beginning in the early stage of children's education when we affirm the innate qualities of children, learn from them, and maintain their loving hearts and trust throughout their education.

PEACE EDUCATION IS CONNECTED TO SPIRITUAL EDUCATION

Being peaceful cannot be separated from being spiritual. Spirituality and peace intertwine. To live in peace is a display of strength, which is not based on external power but inner strength:

> Spiritual practice cultivates inner strength, confidence, inspiration, commitment and sense of purpose. We should address spiritual as well as material poverty.

Only if the scientific civilization can be integrated with the inner spiritual civilization can mutual harmony and an ideal global society be established in the world. Spirituality may nurture moral, ethical and spiritual transformation, which are the keys unlocking the door to our interconnectedness and interdependence. (Lee 2000, p. 167)

Peace is spiritual. The avenue of achieving peace necessarily involves reflective, meditative, and compassionate practices. Materialism and consumerism have resulted in the loss of our "mental equilibrium" (Capra 1999, p. 132), partly because many of us cannot find time to sit down and meditate quietly. We fill our ears with noisy music and jam our stomachs while leaving our souls undernourished. Peace as spiritual growth means a balance between our inner selves and outer selves, between our inner environment and outer environment. It is to create space so that we intensively "hear" the feeling of the heart of all people and are one with the Great Tao.

Transformation of consciousness means for us to be

> . . . learning to be part of the world rather than trying to dominate it—on learning to see rather than merely look, to feel rather than touch, to hear rather than listen: to learn, in short, about the world by being still and opening myself to experiencing it. If I realize that I am an organic part of all that is, and learn to adopt a receptive, connected stance, then I need to take an active, dominant role to understand; the universe will, in essence, include me in understanding. (Delpit 1995, p. 92)

We need to bring meditation back into education, for our students cannot become reflective without looking inward. All the world's great spiritual leaders are meditative persons. Peace education will be more effective when we work on the simultaneous training of the heart, mind, and body, with the parallel cultivation of character and spirit. In cultivating tranquility in the heart and mind, we become more sensitive and begin to allow our higher being to govern our acts.

PEACE EDUCATION AS THE
CONSTRUCTION OF A GLOBAL FAMILY

The peace we are talking about requires a new understanding of human relations:

• True peace must entail humanity's inner solidarity with each other as a species bonded by love. It must be grounded in a new framework in which all human beings are seen as family members living together on the Earth;

- True peace is built upon connection and interconnectedness, sustained by a global ethic of universal love, unconditional forgiveness, and reconciliation.

Violence arises when people are seen as "others" divided from ourselves, and we treat each other as competitors, enemies, opponents, or rivals. The building of true peace means combating biases and breaking down boundaries that divide human beings based on class, gender, race, religious beliefs, and cultural lines. This means humankind taking collective action against hierarchical inequality and transcending all kinds of boundaries so that we connect with each other based on love. We need to know deeply that our destinies as humans are inextricably linked, as we also are with Mother Nature and the universe. As Smith and Carson point out (1998, p. 17), we must see our wholeness; we must also have the humility to listen to each other with our hearts as family members do.

It is from a deep knowing of the interconnectedness and wholeness of our lives that we foster great desire in students to correct social inequalities and injustices in the current world. We realize it is not right for a society to allow a small number of people to control the vast majority of the world's resources while our global family members are deprived of the basic means of survival and dignities of life. Students should feel for others as they feel for themselves and for their family members. At this level of intimacy and connectedness, we could never imagine lifting a gun and pointing it at others.

HUMILITY AND RECONCILIATION AS PEACE EDUCATION

Our world is beautiful because of its rich diversity. To appreciate that all people and existences are remarkable in their own way, we need to have the humility to see all people as our teachers (Jing and Ai 1998). A true sense of humility enables us to see that we can all teach each other something. We learn from negative experiences as well as positive experiences. From such learning arises wisdom.

Reconciliation is action for peace. When we have humility and listen to each other, we have established the preconditions for reconciliation. Reconciliation is to go beyond recognizing our divisions and start the sincere effort of mending and rebuilding relationships. Reconciliation must be taught in school as the springboard to building peace. As Nobel Laureate Desmond Tutu (2004) tells us, we will have no future if we do not forgive.

PEACE EDUCATION AS EDUCATION OF VIRTUE

Peace education cannot avoid being education of virtue. We need to practice virtue in our minds and deeds by embracing love, compassion, forgiveness, piety, repentance, and giving. In the great Chinese philosopher Lao Zi's teaching, virtue is the manifestation of the Great Tao, and the whole universe is harmonized and sustained by the functional principle of virtue. According to Dr. Yan Xin (1996a, 1996b, 1996c), virtue is essential for attaining inner peace and achieving enlightenment. Only when we are able to transcend hatred, anger, separation, jealousy, and greed can our hearts beat in a harmonious manner and our souls' light be rediscovered. Forgiveness is the key to achieving inner peace. Forgiveness frees our hearts from pounding at an abnormal pace; forgiveness stops the exchange of negative energies and intentions between the two parties involved at the subconscious level. Forgiveness gives us the room to view from multiple angles the context, causes, and effects of events.

Furthermore, Dr. Yan Xin holds that virtues are energy-dispersion principles in the universe. When we abide by the principles of love, respect, giving, and forgiveness, we act in sync with the collective spirit of the whole universe. Virtues are mechanisms, structures, methods, and ways to achieve harmonious relationships among nature and social members (Yan Xin 1998). Peace building hence needs to employ education of virtue as the foundational mechanism.

TEACHING SENSITIVITY THROUGH SUBJECT AREAS

Peace education can take place in any subject matter. In teaching history, we can question the notion of war "victories," helping students to realize that victories come with the loss of valuable lives. Maintaining a sense of global family, students are challenged to see that "friends," "allies," and "enemies" are all human beings. Students learn to step into the shoes of others, feeling the loss and pain felt by parents and grandparents, husbands and wives, brothers and sisters, children and friends.

Peace education includes rejecting language that legitimizes violence and wars. Seeing each and every life as divinely valuable, students start to see through the false images projected by terms such as *honor, glory, courage, patriotism, mother of all bombs*, and see the bloody face of *casualties*. Students are given opportunities to see the danger of mobilizing national resources for killing, rather than for building global understanding and deep respect.

Teachers can help students learn about peace through teaching about the efforts of peace leaders and the peace movement. Through stories and facts, students come to an understanding of the power of forgiveness and reconciliation, and feel the hope for peace.

Many educators are promoting multicultural education and transcultural education to help students understand people from diverse backgrounds. These are powerful methods for building cultural respect and understanding. Studying abroad is another highly effective method, for through personal contact and interaction, and by putting a face to a name they start to see others as people who are not, after all, fundamentally different from themselves; rather, students learn we are all human beings sharing very similar concerns and passions. Vivid stories from language textbooks, social studies, history, and children's literature can present life-like scenarios to help children gauge geographical distance and bring their hearts together with other people's. Smith and Carson put it this way:

> Stories and novels help to remove our sense of isolation, because through them we are able to get inside the thoughts and feelings of another person and to see the world through that of another person's eyes. When we can share the experiences of another person, our sense of kinship with the rest of the humanity opens us. By helping individuals to build connections in this way, literature can make an important contribution on world peace. (1998, p. 61)

In all, a key way to cultivate a peace consciousness through subject learning is to help students stop seeing other people as abstract persons, or as negative labels or categories who are grossly dehumanized. Hence, in the classrooms, peace teachers help bring the feeling of personal connection to the forefront of students' attention and awareness. Students learn to see beyond present conflicts, violence, and wars and build up confidence that things can be changed by a new worldview based on global familism, rehumanization, and a total rejection of violence.

The pedagogy of universal love as Nava advocates it (2001) is crucial to the construction of a culture of peace. Teachers can reveal the hidden side of history (Boulding 2000) by finding rich sources of literature to illustrate to students how human beings have loved and cared for each other, and how personal hatred has been overcome through the power of love and forgiveness. Teachers can find a great number of stories in daily life that convey to students effective ways to build understanding and respect. Through teaching and daily interaction, teachers give students the methods, attitude, values, images, and languages to work for peace. In all,

> Peace education is both a philosophy and a process. The philosophy holds values such as trust, caring, empathy, love and a belief in the transformation power

of nonviolence. The process involves the skill of problem-solving, and its inherent components of listening, dialoguing, and seeking mutually beneficial solutions. (Harris and Morrison 2003, p. 207)

TEACHERS AS PEACE EDUCATORS

Our teachers stand in crucial positions to be peace builders. For teachers to become peace educators, a transformation of their awareness and consciousness is necessary. They need to become acutely aware of the current danger humankind is facing; they need to feel a strong calling to change the current situation, and they need to take both small and large actions. The feeling of being called to advocate peace education should come from a deep knowing of our life's purpose and what we need to do at this critical moment in our history. Before teachers begin to teach students sensitivity, they need to develop a sensitivity of their own so they can feel the suffering of all people as beloved brothers and sisters. Peace educators know that actions for peace can be taken at this very moment in our families, schools, and communities. Teachers need to believe in the value and importance of their work, refusing to waver when encountering difficulties and obstacles.

There are many obstacles to becoming a peace educator; for example, teachers are under tremendous pressure to teach the traditional curriculum, which covers war rather than peace (Finley 2003), yet no matter what happens, teachers must "refuse to harden their hearts" (Palmer 1998, p. 1). Peace teachers are required to have tender hearts, to be caring and loving beings. Lao Zi says softness can overcome sharpness. In pursuing peace, it is the tenderness of the heart that overcomes the hardness of hatred.

Teachers are web builders. They enable students to see the web of life that supports us in our daily lives. For example, they can point out that although we do not grow most of our food or make our clothes, we are fed and kept warm because of the labor of others. Peace teachers enable students to see clearly that harming others eventually harms ourselves, and doing good for others eventually leads to good for ourselves.

PEACE EDUCATION AND SOCIETY: MEDIA AND CULTURE

Peace education will be effective only if our society creates a peaceful environment. This includes ensuring the teaching of peace in the mass media and in our culture. We have, as a human race, allowed violent images to invade the souls of our children from a very early age. We have been desensitizing our children to other peoples' humanity, and we have legitimized and justified killing first in the heart and mind, through immersing our children's absorbing minds in violent images and language. Daily exposure to violence has become so routine that we treat it as a commonplace reality (Helman and Hamilton 1989). Violence will have to be totally banned from our mass media and culture before we can implement truly effective peace education. But first and foremost, as educators, we need to denounce all forms of violence in our daily teaching in the classroom, and empower students to refuse violence in the media and all other milieu. Students must be urged to reject "heroes" who perform "rightful" violent killing, oftentimes in a ruthless manner. They are informed that no violence is justified if we wish to have a new beginning for peace.

REDEFINING INTELLIGENCE FOR PEACE

To build sustainable global peace through education, we need to reexamine what makes up our intelligence. Intelligence has been mainly defined as a cognitive function of our brain (Gardner 1993), yet as Nava says,

> It is not possible to separate intelligence from love, compassion, liberty, gratitude, respect, humility, solidarity, friendship, and honesty. Intelligence is an unfolding of one's comprehension of the value of all life and of all human beings. A scientist working for war or a politician who destroy thousands of lives is not intelligent. They may be astute, efficient, and skillful, but they are stupid: They do not know themselves. They are not conscious of what they are doing. Thus, they cannot be considered intelligent. (2001, p. 53)

Unless we teach our children from an early age that we should use our intelligence to love, care, serve, respect, and construct, we are doomed to repeat our mistakes. We hence must connect intelligence with qualities such as love, compassion, gratitude, respect, humility, forgiveness, care, and repentance, to name a few.

We need to posit a new form of intelligence, that is, peace intelligence. Peace intelligence is a form of intelligence that is associated with a deep love for all lives, a deep compassion for all existences, a courage and a conviction for unconditional forgiveness and reconciliation. It is the ability to see others' loss as our own loss, others' pain as our own pain. It is cultivating the ability to coexist in a peaceful, respectful manner. It is an education that expands love in the heart and reduces and eventually eliminates hatred.

DEVELOPING A GLOBAL ETHIC FOR PEACE EDUCATION

Education is in the business of forming new people. It is therefore of vital importance to engage educators in the construction of sustainable global peace. Diverse groups of conscientious teachers and scholars have made efforts to integrate peace education into their teaching. However, as peace education is still marginalized in our education system, individual educators feel powerless in the face of tremendous social, political, and educational obstacles to make peace education empowering and inspiring for themselves and for others. There is a lack of powerful paradigms that would empower teachers to play a critical role in peace building; effective strategies need to be developed to help teachers make peace education an exciting, fulfilling, and professionally enhancing discipline.

Peace education needs to be empowered through constructing a global ethic of universal love, unconditional forgiveness, and reconciliation. This is a vision that brings all of humanity to a common ground, to rally all peace-loving forces to embark on a new beginning to build a peaceful world. The Truth and Reconciliation Commission in South Africa has set us a wonderful example, showing that we can forgive and rebuild our society to reflect true sisterhood and brotherhood (Tutu 1999).

Since the early 1990s, calls have come from around the world to construct a global ethic that would enable world religions and different groups to transcend their differences and work together to bring about long-lasting peace on earth (Kung 1991; Lee 2000). Indeed, our world is in need of a powerful ethic that calls on our higher selves as members of the human race to find the courage and vision to come together and stop all fighting. In other words, unless we embrace a global ethic of universal love, unconditional forgiveness, and reconciliation as a global ethic, we will not be able to have global peace. Based on such a global ethic, we will construct a common ground for all people in the world to hold honest dialogues and begin to treat each other as beloved brothers and sisters. Education holds the hope and carries the responsibility for constructing such a global ethic.

CONCLUSION

We are beings of unity—we share a unity with other human beings, and our body, mind, and spirit are a unity. The separation of these unified aspects in education has taught us severe lessons in the past century. Tomorrow's educators must be peace educators. We need a new generation of educators and a new form of education that brings compassion, love, and understanding back to the fore of educational practice. School must be, first and foremost, a place for learning how to live with love, how to connect, and how to give, forgive, reconcile, and receive with gratitude.

The sustainability of our human race and our integrity as human beings requires our schools to shift their orientation 180 degrees. We need to train our future generations to see into the future. How long can we go on like this? How can we build a global village where we can resolve our problems peacefully? How can we kindle our inner light to fill ourselves with love and peace? These are not just idealistic thoughts, they are necessary, practical questions for us all to consider.

Our oneness with each other and the universe cannot be overemphasized. To live in love and freedom is to be able to connect as well as to give up. We need to work unconditionally for peace and ultimately, "Within One Source and with One Principal, as One Family within One Household, as Co-workers on One Work Place, we can build One Earth Community!" (Lee 2000, p. 170).

Chapter Six

Education for
Human-Nature Harmony

Education for environmental survival and harmony between humans and nature is another challenge that is no longer an option but a necessity. Conscientious individuals and scholars are starting to call for global environmental change, with a sense of urgency (Lin and Ross 2004a, 2004b; Thompson 2000; Hartmann 1999; Milbrath, 1996; Stern et al. 1992; Berry 1988) to discuss environmental education for the 21st century from interdisciplinary perspectives, and to discuss education for ecological renewal (Hutchinson 1998). Feminist scholars are advocating an ecological and nurturing view to center education for love and care (Noddings 1992; Goldstein 1998).

In the 21st century, we need to empower environmental education to deconstruct development paradigms that stress control and manipulation of the environment; there needs to be an inherently environmental and ecological component that promotes a mutually supportive and respectful relationship between humankind and nature.

For too long, we have lost sight of the fact that we are people living in the boat of the planet Earth. We are punching holes in the boat, driving it into dangerous water through humankind's irresponsible behavior. However, we have been fooling ourselves that we can go on like this, and in education this means we have not brought environmental education into the core of our schooling practice. It has to be stressed that there is no time to lose for us to cultivate a strong sense of responsibility and reciprocity in our relationship with nature. We need to emphasize the critical importance of instilling habits of humility and frugality in our lives to ensure our survival and sustainability.

Nava (2001) calls for a new form of eco-education:

Eco-education tells us that the natural world is an extension of ourselves: We form part of a living world. The world is not something separated from us. We

71

must care for our world, because it contains limited resources, and if these resources are exhausted, humankind's very survival will be in jeopardy. Our world, which is the great classroom where the child learns, is currently suffering from an extremely pronounced destruction of its natural resources. If this trend continues, children will only see a clean river or a forest in a video or movie, because all the rivers and forests will be polluted or dried up. The relationship of the student with nature is crucial, and is the foundation of any relevant education for our times. It must be remembered that the welfare of a culture depends upon the relation it is capable of establishing with the earth. Thus, eco-education establishes a new relation with the natural world. (p. 100)

Education in the 21st century must support a view of interdependence and advocate a new lifestyle that sustains rather than exhausts natural resources. Integrating environmental education into the mainstream of educational theory and practice is critical in the 21st century.

Criteria for excellence need to be changed as well. A good education must also include ecological and environmental studies that enable students to see the deep connection between all existences in the universe. Such education cultivates a profound understanding of the reciprocity of humanity and nature. A good student is one who can contribute to the preservation and sustainability of our Mother Earth; a good teacher is an environmental protectionist and an effective advocate as well.

ENVIRONMENTAL EDUCATION CURRICULUM

We are living in a huge classroom for environmental education if we adjust our view to see nature and the universe as our school. We should introduce Earth as our precious home to students from the beginning of their schooling, enabling them to see a holistic picture of where they live and to think about its protection and sustainability.

In the early stage of education, we can encourage students to observe the harmonious working of the universe, for example, to observe how the stars revolve around each other, how life forms sustain each other. Students' curiosity about nature, the universe, and life should be encouraged and captured as opportunities to understand the interconnectedness of the universe. Students *have* the wisdom to comprehend the wholeness of the universe if we encourage them in their quest for it. As stated earlier, they comprehend the universe as a whole. They see the world in connections. They see divinity in everything. Students should feel that it is normal to ask questions, and they should be encouraged to use their imaginations to understand the world and the universe as an intelligent system as well as from an organic perspective.

Our students need to understand the serious problems we face, such as global warming, ozone layer depletion, air and water pollution, desertification, poverty, and social injustice. Students should be informed about how we are all part of the problems, and in order to make change, we need to start changing ourselves, including our lifestyles and mentality.

For example, we need to inform our students that over 1500 acres of land are becoming desert worldwide every hour, largely because of the destruction of upwind forests. Rainforests are called the "lungs of earth," yet every minute seventy-two acres of rainforests are destroyed, mostly by impoverished people who are cutting and burning the forest to create agricultural or pasture lands to grow beef for export to the United States (Hartman 1999, pp. 48–50). "This 38 million-acres-per-year loss will wipe out the entire world's rainforests in our children's lifetimes if it continues at its current pace. The end, literally, is within sight" (p. 50).

ENVIRONMENTAL EDUCATION AND TEACHING INNOVATION

Environmental education carries great potential to connect theory with practice, and knowledge with practical use. In an ecological environmental education classroom, students are encouraged to identify problems, conduct collaborative or independent research, analyze policies and practices that have worked or gone wrong, and design programs that help solve environmental problems in their community. Through students' and educators' efforts to engage in the actual acts of "doing" environmental education, students develop a sense of efficacy and cultivate their ability to effect social changes. Their creativity is cultivated along with their social imagination. Their moral, intellectual, emotional, ecological, and spiritual values are shaped in the process.

ENVIRONMENTAL EDUCATION AS FRUGALITY EDUCATION

The importance of acquiring the habit of frugality cannot be overemphasized. Environmental education should start with students learning to forego the habit of waste. Any food, any piece of paper should be treasured. Second, we need to help students forego the obsession with possession. A mentality of custodianship needs to be cultivated in which students see their role as caretakers of the Earth's resources rather than possessors of them. They must see that our resources are not inexhaustible, and that all of us have the obligation to be careful with everything we use and consume.

ENVIRONMENTAL EDUCATION AS HUMILITY EDUCATION

A sense of humility needs to be cultivated in our students. The sense of humility arises from knowing that we are dependent on our natural environment for survival. It arises from a deep knowing that nature has its own laws, and violating them will bring us destruction. It also comes from an intuition that all lives are intelligent, and we can learn an incredible amount of wisdom and knowledge from all existences about how to survive and balance. When we are humble and respectful, we accept our limitations and become appreciative and capable of listening to the warnings of nature and the voice of wisdom for solutions.

ENVIRONMENTAL EDUCATION AS GRATITUDE EDUCATION

Gratitude is an important attribute we want to cultivate in students. Students are urged not to take for granted that they have food on the table and clothes to wear, that the sun gives us light, trees give us oxygen, and parents bring us up with selfless giving and love. Gratitude gives rise to a feeling of nature as our mother, Earth as our cradle, our boat in the ocean of the universe. Gratitude education brings students to the realization of how privileged we have been, and how much we need to appreciate and reciprocate.

ENVIRONMENTAL EDUCATION AS HOLISTIC EDUCATION

Environmental education can be combined with the teaching of philosophy, math, science, and social sciences. Nature is a vast encyclopedia that requires us to teach it using a holistic learning style. We need to put our souls, minds, hearts, and bodies together to understand our environment. Environmental education should be education without walls. Acquiring knowledge, developing practical skills, cultivating socially responsible imaginations, and cultivating virtues such as care and compassion should characterize a holistic environmental education.

ENVIRONMENTAL EDUCATION AS WISDOM EDUCATION

Environmental education should be wisdom education. Students are encouraged to learn from the wisdom of Native Americans, Canadians, and Australians; from indigenous people around the world; from Taoism and

Buddhism; and from eco-feminism, to name just a few. In all, wisdom is richly embedded in many cultures and traditions that instruct us deeply and wisely about the relationship between humans and nature.

Human-nature harmony and mutual sustainability mean we align our consciousness with the will of all. As we have argued, human consciousness is to be understood not only as thoughts and ideas flowing through the brain, but it is also a medium carrying tremendous energy, information, and material-based transformational power. Every moment, we are exchanging energy, matter, and information with all forms of existences through our thoughts. In order to function in synchronicity with the consciousness/energy of the universe, we need to give up the notion of human centrality and place ourselves in equal relation to all that exists in the universe. In the process of giving love and care to all sentient and nonsentient beings, as Buddhism calls them, we receive vital life support and energy from all. This give-and-take relationship functions in complex and subtle ways that underlie the balance, harmony, and sustainability of the universe.

Chinese Taoist tradition focuses on cultivating energy to transform the body, mind, and spirit to form a new being who is enlightened and becomes one with the Great Tao. For them, virtuous thoughts and deeds attract positive energy, whereas negative thoughts and deeds beget negative energy. Inherently, human beings can connect with and transform the natural environment in a positive way, by not seeing ourselves as the center of the universe and by working with the will of all and for the good of all that exists. Only when we love unconditionally do we receive reciprocal, unconditional support in the form of energy from people and all that exists. The kindness in our hearts toward each other and all things must be genuine, sincere, selfless, and unconditional.

ENVIRONMENTAL EDUCATION AS ANTIGREED EDUCATION

In Buddhist teachings, greed comes from attachment (to material goods), and attachment comes from a sense of separation, which comes from a lack of understanding of the truth of the universe. In today's era of globalization, capitalism has been touted as the model of development for the whole world. Capitalism as a social and economic system encourages people to chase profits and fulfill their desires as quickly as possible. Short-term views are used to judge the health of an economy or a company. Capitalism also defines human relationships in terms of haves and have-nots, and consumerism and materialism take precedent over our emotional, moral, and spiritual well-being. Wealth and power become the most important scriteria for evaluating the value and success of a human being. Defining our relationships with each other and with nature only in terms of utilitarianism, we see others as opponents rather than family members having a shared existence on Earth. We perform acts of aggression toward each other, and to get more and more, we scorch our land and butcher animals without the faintest sense of guilt—even though we know their crying is full of pain and horror. Destruction and imbalance in the environment have led to floods, storms, droughts, deforestation, and the extinction of countless species, and in 2004, a deadly tsunami, killing more than 250,000 people. Yet the most highly educated people on Earth, our scientists and social scientists, often say little and allow all of these to happen.

One reason for all these behaviors is that most people believe that material things will bring them true happiness. As Roger Walsh states,

> Our culture is fixated on the physical foursome of money, sensuality, power and prestige—we are lost in the seductive illusion that if we can somehow just get enough of them, we will finally be fully and forever happy. (1999, p. 32)

Hence, antigreed education has to be connected with an education about what truly brings us happiness. This requires an adjustment of life attitudes, values, and habits. A deep knowing should be developed—that is, we cannot "possess" material wealth—we are entrusted with it for only a short time and cannot take it away when we leave the world. As Lao Zi says, too much material possession is a hindrance to freedom: "When there is too much gold in the house, we lose the freedom to travel far." Furthermore, too much concern with material possessions takes our attention away from seeking wisdom from within. Greed can eat away our compassion. It can lead to the destruction of our environment without any consideration of the consequences. Therefore, an authentic form of environmental education is antigreed education.

ENVIRONMENTAL EDUCATION AS EXPERIENTIAL LEARNING

Experiences are powerful tools for helping students to acquire environmental awareness and sensitivity. Students need to feel and experience the Earth as a living organism and as a being alive with emotions. Students may learn more if, for example, teachers

- take students to see a glorious sunrise;
- engage students in an environmental protection activity;

- encourage students to hug a tree, to talk with plants and animals; and
- urge students to imagine and experience the feelings of plants and animals.

These activities will affirm students' feelings and strengthen their identification with nature. They will feel a personal connection and develop an experiential sensitivity to all that exists in the world.

TRANSCENDING PATRIARCHAL VALUES AND REDISCOVERING WOMEN'S WISDOM

Our world is still governed by masculine values and remnants of patriarchal traditions. Women, who tend to see the world in a connected, interdependent, nurturing manner, have been marginalized in international and national policy making on environmental protection. "Feminine" traits such as caring, support, and connection have been deemed traits of lower quality. To adopt a paradigm of stewardship and interdependce between humans and nature, we must reconstruct "feminine traits" as key virtues for sustaining and maintaining the balance and harmony between nature and humankind. We need a new mode of social inquiry and a profoundly different path for human and social development.

In the patriarchal system, men have dominated in all aspects of society. Women were subjected to all kinds of discrimination, and their lives were defined in terms of serving their husbands and children. Women had no political, economic, or intellectual voice. Feminine and masculine attributes were polarized. Women were seen as loving, caring, dependent, spiritual, intuitive, weak, and obedient, while men were associated with aggressiveness, innovation, determination, independence, success, and rationality. Women were considered the lesser half of the human race, and feminine traits ascribed to women were treated as weaknesses.

Since the middle of the 20th century, women have struggled for comprehensive equality with men, and these struggles can be briefly placed into several theoretical frameworks (Tong 1989). In liberal feminism, women demanded equality in political participation and educational and employment opportunities. Marxist feminism went further, employing a critical framework in examining the foundation of the social economic structure that devalued women's reproductive work and deprived women of economic independence. Radical feminism questions the imposition of femininity on women and masculinity on men, and the designation of male and female roles into public and private domains. In postmodern feminism, the concept of man as the person and the woman as the other has been critically examined; feminist scholars call for restoring women's history and identity and developing a new discourse and epistemology that recognizes diversity and plurality in experiences and voices. In all, women aspire to be equal with men.

However, the core culture of most societies remains largely unchanged. Culture in today's society still underscores the profound devaluation of women and many other groups, such as ethnic minorities, as equal human beings. As Belenky and her colleagues (1986) argue, values and ways of knowing in Western core culture and in educational institutions "have been shaped throughout history by the male-dominated majority culture. Drawing on their own perspective and visions, men have constructed the prevailing theories, written history, and set values that have become the guiding principles for men and women alike" (p. 5).

Eco-feminism, which emerged in the past two decades, claiming that the patriarchal male model of social development has led to disastrous environmental conditions, calls for a return to our union with Mother Nature and adoption of a harmonious, rather than a controlling, relationship with nature. Eco-feminism ponders the relationship between human and nature under patriarchal society (Tong 1998; Plant 1989). Essentially, eco-feminism posits that we got into the trouble we are in today precisely because we have adopted a patriarchal strategy or paradigm in understanding the relationship between human beings and nature. The Earth was considered feminine, to be conquered, exploited, penetrated, and used up. The past 2000 years of human history follow what we could say was essentially a masculine patriarchal paradigm for social and economic development.

The domination of the patriarchal masculine paradigm has conditioned our consciousness and our views on the world and nature. Although women in the last fifty years have made important inroads into social, economic, cultural, political, and educational sectors, our ways of understanding the world have not changed. For example, in science and social science there is still a serious polarization of concepts such as feminine/masculine, subjective/objective, rational/intuitive, and so on, and male perspectives dominate discourse in social development and human nature.

Thinking in science today essentially treats the human body, mind, and spirit as separated. Feminine and masculine qualities are taken as distinctly separated from each other and indeed deemed as exclusive of each other. The mechanistic Newtonian view of the world "shortchanged the universe by reducing it to a secular machine, describing it as operating only according to unwavering mechanistic laws" (Redfield 1997, p. xxii). In the scientific world, "any contention that there is an active spiritual force in the universe or that higher spiritual experience is anything other than hallucination was too often dismissed out of hand (p. xxii.) Science and technology have become the new religion of the world that prizes value-free, emotion-free rationality, "predictability," repeatability, and objectivity above values, emotions, spirit, and intuition. Scientific "laws" are considered universal and unchallengeable, and human beings and nature are studied as isolated, alienated, and disjointed parts. Humans are treated as means, not as ends—the attention to the emotional, moral, and spiritual reality of our existence is reduced to the minimum; and human beings are place above all lives and objects on Earth.

In social science, social development theories, from the theory of evolution to modernization theory, from functional theory to human capital theory, center their attention on ruthless competition for resources on Earth in the name of growth and progress. Development models reinforce human-centeredness and individualism, and an insatiable greed for bigger and more, which foster a consumerism and materialism based on greed. In the dominance of scientific objectivity, social science subjects are studied with little regard to our feelings and spirits, or our interconnectedness as human beings and with nature. Spiritual development is dismissed by most social scientists as a closed subject, for it is immeasurable by modern equipment and unverifiable. Social services and prestige are distributed according to this line:

> Western society has traditionally favored the male side rather than the female. Instead of recognizing that the personality of each man and of each woman is the result of an interplay between female and male elements, it has established a static order where all men are supposed to be masculine and all women feminine, and it has given men the leading roles and most of society's privileges. This attitude has resulted in an over-emphasis of all the yang—or male—aspects of human nature: activity, rational thinking, competition, aggressiveness, and so on. The yin—or female—modes of consciousness, which can be described by words like intuitive, religious, mystical, occult or psychic, have constantly been oppressed in our male oriented society. (Capra 1999, p. 147–148)

In sum, the prevailing mode of inquiry in science and social sciences has been male constructed and dominated. In the striving toward objectivity, subjectivity is greatly devalued. Personal feelings are discounted. This means direct and personal experiences are dismissed as powerful ways of knowing. It means turning a blind eye to the pain of nature's sufferings and the crying of Mother Earth; it means we pretend to know it all while we know in our souls that something is fundamentally wrong; despite many horrible warnings, we continue to fail to wake up and undergo a "conscious evolution" toward a higher civilization based on love and harmony.

The Complementariness of Yin and Yang: Eastern Wisdom on Virtues and Human-Nature Relationship

The theory of the creation of the universe as extrapolated in the *Tao Te Ching* sees that the universe was originally a big void. From the void evolved the original qi—which is the fundamental element that unifies all things and people in the universe. The Original qi divides into two, the yin and yang energy, which interact and copulate to create the three, namely heaven, Earth, and people, and from the three emerge a myriad of things. So the original qi, which has the combined quality of matter, energy, bio/eco-information, and spirit, is in everything in the universe. It is the unifying force that lets all existences function in harmony in the universe. Human beings and all existences are open systems, forever engaging in the exchange of the original qi. In the creation of all lives and things, yang is the energy that creates and motivates, and yin is the energy that nourishes, nurtures, sustains, and harmonizes. Yin and yang are complementary and indispensable to each other; their dynamic interplay formulates great diversity in humans and nature, all of which contains the energy of yin and yang. Yin and yang are not absolute. Yin contains the element of yang, and yang contains the element of yin. Yang recedes cyclically to yin, which when it reaches its fullness, recedes to yang. The balance of yin and yang preconditions the harmonious existence of nature and human beings; the disruption of such a balance leads to too much yang or too much yin, either of which can cause problems in our natural environment and in our bodies, even great natural disasters.

Our natural environment is formed of yin and yang energy. The sun spreads yang energy, while the moon disperses yin energy. The sun also contains an element of yin energy, and the moon also has an element of yang energy. Our bodies are also an embodiment of the yin and yang force. According to Traditional Chinese Medicine, our upper body is yang, and the lower body is yin; our front part is yang, and back is yin; our inner body is yin, and our outer body is yang. Our heart contains the energy of yang (fire), while our kidney stores the energy of yin (water). Deep breathing brings these two energies together that create nutrient qi, which flows through the body's meridians (qi's energy path) to provide vital, primordial energy to nurture our organs.

The above implies that male and female, yin and yang, are not separated from each other. Rather, we are connected in energy, matter, and spirit. We embody each other. Both women and men can be loving, strong, independent, dependent, and caring at the same time.

Virtues form the foundation of the whole universe so it can function in a coordinated, well-balanced, and harmonious manner. Because we all come from the same source of spirit/matter/energy, we and all that exist are family members on the Earth. We are not here to conquer and exploit one another and Mother Nature. We need to rely on virtues, or socially defined feminine qualities, such as caring and love and compassion, to transcend hatred, anger, jealousy, and greed. Virtues are not just moral beliefs that belong only to the private domain, but rather they are functional, energy-driven techniques, mechanisms, and structures that are working every day to maintain harmony in the universe. The universe functions with an underlying principle of virtue. Everything is interrelated in a reciprocal, loving, giving relationship. All creatures in the universe need to engage in selfless giving, in an exchange of energy, information, material substance, and spirit.

To summarize, we should not see feminine virtues as belonging only to the female, nor treat feminine traits as inferior. We need a balanced world—women need to play key roles in the protection of our Mother Earth, and education needs to reflect this truth.

Virtue as the Foundation of Our Existence

Taking virtue as the foundation of the universe and adopting virtues as key qualities in our existence (Yan Xin 1996b, 1996c, 1996d) suggests a new paradigm for the possibility of our connecting with the heart and soul of everything and every being in the universe. It gives us a tool to "break with the mechanical and the routine," and do what "appeal[s] to us in our freedom, to our sense that things ought to be, and can be otherwise" (Greene 1993, p. 214). This new perspective sets us free from the patriarchal obsession with control and launches us onto the path of being love-giving people and healers. The notion of yin-yang balance sheds light on how we should take women's voices out of silence and deconstruct "paradigms throughout our culture that function deliberately to repress, to belittle other ways of being, and sometimes to make those alternative ways appear threatening, requiring censorship or prohibition or even a violent demise" (p. 216).

Reconstructing femininity and masculinity calls for refocusing on key issues facing humankind based on the broadest vision and greatest compassion. This necessitates bringing the marginalized into the center. As bell hooks says,

> Living as we did, on the edge, we developed a particular way of seeing reality. We looked from the outside in and from the inside out. We understood both. This mode of seeing reminded us of the existence of a whole universe, a main body made up of both margin and center. Our survival depended on an ongoing public awareness of the separation between margin and center and an ongoing private acknowledgment that we were a necessary, vital part of the whole. This sense of wholeness, impressed upon our consciousness by the structure of our daily lives, provided us with an oppositional world view—a mode of seeing unknown to most of our oppressors that sustained us, aided us in our struggle to

transcend poverty and despair, strengthened our sense of self and solidarity. (1990, p. 149)

It is time that we realign our minds and deeds back to a balanced state so that we can build a more balanced and sustainable world. We all know that our environment has suffered a lot of problems—polluted air, polluted water, soil erosion, deforestation, desertification, and so on. All of these problems are causing major destruction. We also know that there is a big hole in the ozone layer at the North Pole. Now this is also appearing at the South Pole. Realizing that we are connected in energy, matter, and spirit with all other ecospecies on Earth, we cannot treat the Earth as only something to be conquered, to be exploited, and to be used up. Knowing that we are all linked with the same energy of the universe's creation, and that we all rely on each other for survival, we need to formulate a new human and social relationship based on the centrality of virtue. We *must* move toward a more advanced and civilized society where there would be no wars, aggression, great devastation, sufferings, or bitterness. Failing this will lead to our extinction. It is time for us to achieve the balance between the so-called feminine and masculine, subjective and objective, human and nature, to achieve the balance between yin and yang, based on virtue. It is time for us to integrate every aspect of our lives with love, compassion, forgiveness, and repentance for the common good.

Together with everything else in the universe, we form unity:

> The most important characteristic of the Eastern world view—one could almost say the essence of it—is the awareness of the unity and mutual interrelation of all things and events, the experience of all phenomena in the world as manifestations of a basic oneness. All things are seen as interdependent and inseparable parts of this comic whole, as different manifestations of the same ultimate reality. The Eastern traditions refer to this ultimate, indivisible reality which manifests itself in all things, and of which all things are parts. It is called *Brahman* in Hinduism, *Dharmakaya* in Buddhism, *Tao* in Taoism. (Capra 1999, pp. 130–131)

The balance of yin and yang means the conservation of energy. It means a balanced condition that allows growth and restoration, exchanges and creation:

> To achieve such a dynamic state of balance, a radically different social and economic structure will be needed: a cultural revolution in the true sense of the word. The survival of our whole civilization may depend on whether we can bring about such a change. It will depend, ultimately, on our ability to adopt some of the *yin* attitudes of Eastern mysticism; to experience the wholeness of nature and the art of living with it in harmony. (Capra 1999, p. 307)

The dilemma we are in begs us to consider the notion of development based on masculine values:

> In the global context, the term *development* has been used to rank countries as developed, developing, or underdeveloped based on various indicators and indices. Most are economic; they measure the output of goods and services, income, money supply, and so on. Simultaneously, there is some concern with poverty and unequal distribution of wealth. The developed countries provide the yardstick by which all other countries are ranked. (Jain 2000, p. 45)

Jain argues that the concept of development has been used to describe only forms of economic growth. Development is equated with mass mechanization and industrialization, high levels of production of goods and services, super affluence in material goods, high energy consumption, and so on. She thus urges an alternative form of development, which is the growth of people's capacities and strengths, of their public involvement and their self-reliance, and of their equal status. Jain's arguments are powerful, but we need to go further. We need to debunk the concept of development that has resulted in the extinction of animals and plants, causing holes in our ozone layer and polluting our air with poisonous elements. The whole notion underscoring capitalism that success means greedily chasing profits and developing technology without an equivalent consciousness about its responsible use must be reevaluated.

The universe has expressed its love to us unconditionally. What we need is to listen with our hearts. Inherently, our hearts are connected with all that exists based on support and trust. We cannot afford to break up that support and trust. We must develop a new world view, a new philosophy, a new epistemology, a new science that give justice back to emotions, feelings, intuition, to our spiritual essence. Masculinity or yang without femininity, or yin without yang, does not reflect our true existence.

UNIVERSAL LOVE AND OUR ENVIRONMENTAL SURVIVAL

We must perform every act out of love for people and things and return our natural environment to balance and sustainability. We must love our environment as we love ourselves. As Palmer (1993) says,

> A knowledge that springs from love will implicate us in the web of life; it will wrap the knower and the known in compassion, in a bond of awesome responsibility as well as transforming joy; it will call us to involvement, mutuality, accountability. (p. 9)

A holistic understanding of human relationship with nature should enable us to hear the voices of the natural world, and together play a song of life with the universe. As Berry (1988) puts it,

> Presently we are returning to the primordial community of the universe, the earth, and all living things. Each has its own voice, its role, its power over the whole. But, most important, each has its special symbolism. The excitement of life is in the numinous experience wherein we are given to each other in that larger celebration of existence in which all things attain their highest expression, for the universe, by definition, is a single gorgeous celebratory event. (p. 5)

Chapter Seven

Education for Wisdom: A Paradigm Shift in Educational Reform

THE GREAT NEGLECT OF CURRENT REFORM INITIATIVES

There is a great neglect in the current debate on educational reform. Currently, while the debates center upon improving school achievement through standardization and accountability, questions concerning the deeper purpose of school reforms are seldom discussed, such as, What are the most urgent needs in our society today? What kind of world do we want to build for the future through education? Is what we are doing connected with what we believe we should be doing as educators? What direction is education taking down the road?

Globally, school reforms have been dominated by the quest for competitiveness. The current debate on school reform has been guided by a functionalist perspective, which assumes that the goal of reform is neutral, that it will serve society by improving the efficiency of the education system. In the intensive push for competitiveness, schools strive at jamming more and more information into students' minds, while little has been said about how students should use the knowledge and information responsibly and wisely. Learning becomes predominantly about the things "out there," rather than about a quest for wisdom, the thirst for learning.

Educational reform of the heart, for the good of all humanity, and for the benefit of all existences, is needed in the 21st century. Educational reform must be envisioned with a picture of a better world in mind. Hence, reform efforts should be about wisdom and should be guided by wisdom. We need to focus on giving children values and skills to chart their life course and to help them build a peaceful and ecologically sustainable world. We need to turn away from teaching students to see that nature is only an object for conquest.

We will equip students with the will and ability to say no to violent games and movies. We will talk openly about values that are dear to our hearts and souls and throw away the pretense of moral relativism, knowing that there are right choices and wrong choices for us to make, and right choices lead us to a loving and peaceful world.

Massive misunderstandings among people and cultures have built up. It is wisdom-guided reform that will lead us to find solutions. Until we engage in a soul-searching debate on how we should remake our future, education as the enterprise of cultivating future global citizens won't effect profound changes in our world for the common good.

In today's highly materialist world, we educators are challenged to talk among ourselves and with our students about how we should handle human desires, how we can transcend greed and live within our means. We should discuss what true sources of joy are, and how to handle suffering and take advantage of difficult situations for spiritual growth. We can enlighten our students with the knowledge that what is happening "out there" has to do with what we are doing "in here." A wisdom-guided education finds it not only pertinent but extremely important to discuss the meaning of life with ourselves and our students. Educators must refuse to develop a hardened heart through the dictatorship of "professional objectivity" and take up the whole range of life issues in their professional inquiry.

THE ESSENCE OF EDUCATION FOR WISDOM

Education in the 21st century cannot help but be about wisdom. How can we help our students develop wisdom? This will eventually be the central question in future educational reform debates.

Education for wisdom urges us to go beyond learning skills and gaining knowledge, to start learning about and living the experience of love, compassion, respect, forgiveness, and understanding. It is a about "reclaiming goodness" (Alexander 2001). Currently, we are scared of talking about values and virtues, or reluctant to bring them into the center of our discussion because they are treated as intangible, subjective, and religiously or politically laden values. However, as educators realize that these values and virtues are indispensable qualities for students' success in life and for society's well-being, a different educational paradigm will hopefully emerge. Furthermore, they are essential for humanity's survival and sustainability. By putting aside wisdom education and emphasizing skills and knowledge, we are letting the cart drive the horse, and we are depriving ourselves of a truly educative experience.

In the face of global crises such as unrest, environmental breakdown, poverty, health problems, and a serious moral breakdown in our society, we will not be able to start building a new future if our students are trained to think of themselves as separate individuals. Although our education trumpets cooperative learning, team building. and so on, we have not insisted on cultivating in students a big mind and a big heart to think and feel for all of humankind, for the coexistence of nature and humanity. By ignoring the development of wisdom, we have brought up generations of people who condone wars openly or silently, who support leaders and join the march to kill even though we know the so-called enemies are just people like us. Social inequality is perpetuated because we consider some people "justified" in having billions of dollars while others can barely survive. In many ways, we have substituted our social conscience and inherent sense of equality with acceptance of inequality due to the lack of wisdom education.

How Do We Acquire Wisdom?

Education for wisdom involves a major paradigm shift in our debate on educational reform. Wisdom comes from all sources. We can learn wisdom from world cultures, traditions, and religions. Native people and indigenous cultures hold deep insights about the secrets of life. They have maintained their perennial wisdom about how to maintain the intricate balance between humankind and nature; they know how to get into the hearts and souls of animals, flowers, stones:

> The indigenous tribes of South America, North America, Africa, Australia, and early Asia . . . lived a sustainable way of life, seeing the sacredness of the world and the presence of the Creator and divinity in all things, and generally led fulfilling lives with far more leisure time than working-class citizens of the industrialized world will ever enjoy. (Hartmann 1999, p. 3)

In the *Book of Changes*, which contains sixty-four archetypal patterns of relationships between humans, nature, and the universe, ancient Chinese sages illustrate the virtue of humility with the symbol of a mountain below the Earth. This symbolizes that if one is able to lower one's ego, one forever receives knowledge and wisdom. Lao Zi teaches us that water can become an ocean because it is willing to stay in lowly places and accept all water that comes in. Buddhist teachings in texts such as *The Diamond Sutra* inform us that a person's ultimate enlightenment is a realization that all of us are equal, and all existences are equal, that becoming a great person like the Buddha requires one to shed all ego and be willing to be unconditionally passionate to help all existences reach enlightenment.

We can learn from a flying bird and an opening rose; we can learn from our grandmas and grandpas, who may be illiterate but who exemplify a life of unconditional love and giving. Wisdom is not a set of complex formulas, but oftentimes is simple truth. Wisdom comes from living what we should be: compassionate, caring, selfless, loving, forgiving, respectful, honest, integral, humble, and so on. Wisdom calls for us to explore our true self—what religions call the God in us, the Buddha seed, the Tao in us, where wisdom resides. This requires removing illusions of separation and connecting with the boundless collective intelligence of which we are all a part.

Wisdom cannot be separated from virtue. As Plato states in his *Republic*, knowledge and virtues are to be connected, and the combination gives rise to wisdom. Knowledge without virtue is like a ship without guidance. Only when the two are intimately connected does one have wisdom.

Educators Becoming Seekers of Wisdom

When we stress that education is for the cultivation of wisdom, the dynamics of education change. The job of educators and researchers is no longer just teaching or researching, but to become seekers, going beyond obsession with neutrality and rationality to actively engage our intuition, our souls, and hearts in the whole process of teaching and learning. We are searching for wisdom from the outside world as well as within our hearts and souls. Students and teachers are open to learning about all that is in life and in the cosmos. They help each other to awaken the deep power of love within themselves and to become more creative and imaginative than they think they can ever be.

Teachers as wisdom seekers put their souls into their students and their subjects—teaching engages a teacher's soul (Palmer 1998, p. 9). Teachers engage students in the exploration of existential questions and urge students to go beyond personal interests to work for the good of others and for the common good. They encourage their students to see obstacles as opportunities to test their resolve to love, forgive, and reconcile. Teachers as wisdom seekers, therefore, strengthen their commitment to love and wisdom through these kinds of endeavors.

Transforming Ourselves before We Transform the World

A true reform in education should not be transforming something "out there," but something "in here." Have we maintained a fresh sensitivity for the world's suffering? Have we recently given hope to people who are searching in the dark? True reformers are those who take great pains to transform themselves before they transform others. We transform in order to reform.

Self-transformation comes with a constant reflection on who we are, what we are doing, and whether we are making the world a better or worse place. These questions set us on the process of transformation. Wisdom arises when we seek teachers in books and our surrounding environment. Wisdom cannot be separated from our virtue. When we learn to be loving and forgiving, we know what wisdom is. *Wisdom is to be lived.* It is a state of being. It is only through this kind of living wisdom that one can hope to transform others. Wisdom seekers are consciously creating an existence larger than themselves, reaching out to embrace others as their own dear ones. It is in being included, trusted, loved, and forgiven that others are transformed.

ACADEMIC SCHOLARSHIP

Can we challenge ourselves to come out of our narrow professional domains and work together for a new future? Can we forgo the pretense of objectivity and speak from our hearts? Can we require ourselves to be first and foremost givers of love and compassion? Scholars are being challenged to think about these questions. Academics have been privileged by having a great deal of autonomy to pursue the secrets of the world. But compartmentalization has narrowed our vision and restricted our ability to effect changes in how society resolves our major crises.

Academics have shied away from researching about how love, care, compassion, and forgiveness can functionally and structurally improve our schools and society. With the rational, mechanistic framework that guides research today, we fear studying ourselves as whole persons, as this framework takes love and other virtues as "mushy, fuzzy, subjective, personal, loaded. In a word, unresearchable" (Goldstein 1998, p. 8). Goldstein laments,

> No one has turned the lens of scholarly inquiry to focus on the dimensions and nature of teacherly love because wise scholars tend to shy away from unresearchable research topics. Love is difficult to define, impossible to measure, and outside the boundaries of generalizability, reliability, and validity. Why bother? (p. 8)

Goldstein calls for teachers to practice "living loving teaching," to combine teaching with love. This is a great challenge and vision for us to live up to. We need to go further and combine academic research with love. A researcher needs to see love as a great force in the universe, which has everything to do with fulfillment of our life goals and our professional achievement, and which is inherently part of our pursuit of a better world.

THE WISDOM CLASSROOM

We should examine school curriculum and ask these questions: Are the subjects we teach enabling our students to love and care for each other and for the well-being of nature? Does the teaching of history and other subjects contain ultranationalism or glorification of killing in the name of patriotism? Does the teaching of geography limit our minds to regionalism? Does the teaching of science deny our spirituality? Does the language we use inside and outside the classroom give students a positive mindset and a peaceful vocabulary?

In a wisdom classroom, there is discussion on major problems facing our society. There is criticism of the irrational act of spending hundreds of billions on the building of weapons for killing each other, while a huge number of people live in poverty and have no medical care. Educators must boldly imagine a new kind of social structure, one that gives all people quality education and universal healthcare, one that leads to the elimination of poverty and discrimination, and one that gives all people dignity and respect as equal souls.

WISDOM-BASED TEACHER TRAINING

It is important for our future to have teachers who have received wisdom-based teacher training. Currently, we focus mainly on transmitting to our prospective teachers knowledge and skills in different subject areas so that they can impart them to their students. Knowledge transmission and classroom management skills are stressed. However, knowledge is often taught without the engagement of the hearts and souls of teacher education students. The attributes of universal love, unconditional forgiveness, and respect are not being cultivated as an indispensable, inherent part of what makes a great teacher in our teacher education programs. Teachers are expected to refine the skill of teaching subject contents, but seldom are they expected to develop big hearts to elevate all students morally and spiritually, helping them to become constructive workers for a peaceful and equal world. All in all, we emphasize that teachers possess an exceptional amount of knowledge, but not an exceptional amount of love and compassion to be imparted to their students.

So teacher education programs should not only teach subject-matter knowledge but, more importantly, treat the acquisition of qualities such as compassion and love as major tasks in teacher training.

EDUCATORS AS WISDOM TEACHERS

Teachers' roles should be those of soul guide, supporter, friend, student, mentor, and role model. The teaching profession should be treated as one's calling to care and love and to give our world hope through the nurturing of new beings. Teachers should see their work as part of the human collective effort in the quest for peace, sustainability, and enlightenment. When teachers see their work in this way, they embark on the journey as wisdom teachers.

Wisdom teachers see learners as those walking with them on the same path of soul development and social advancement. They believe not only that all students can learn, but also that students have something to teach them. A student with an academic challenge provides an opportunity for teachers to learn how to offer a helping hand and be persistent with a positive expectation. A wisdom teacher challenges students with exceptional learning ability to cultivate big hearts to help others so that all are glorified with the joy of learning.

In all, learning is reciprocal. It flows not only from teachers to students but also from students to teachers, from student to student, community to school, and school to community. Interaction between individual students and teachers goes way beyond the explication of text materials. Teachers see learning as a holistic endeavor. Students' emotional, moral, intellectual, and spiritual development are all taken into consideration.

When evaluating students, wisdom teachers do not judge students based simply on the correct or incorrect answers they put down on an exam paper or home assignment. Rather, they see learning as a process, and keeping up with a schedule is not as great a concern as the learning of values and traits that are based on the importance of love. Teachers do not punish students based on the number of correct answers; rather, they see incorrect answers as a need for help. They always see beauty in children, regardless of their grades; they appreciate them for who they are, as inherently equal souls who come together to learn and grow.

NEW PERSPECTIVES ON KNOWLEDGE, NEW LEARNING APPROACHES

In education for wisdom, learning is not limited to the subjects we have set up in today's schools. What is considered knowledge includes our quest for life's purpose and the natural world as a dynamic and living system that interacts with the human world. Knowledge also includes those aspects of learning that touch on human morality and human spirituality. Knowledge should include our responsibility to each other as a global family, to support each other for our common survival and prosperity. Knowledge and skills are not just formulas to be applied to physical reality; more importantly, they are to be applied for humanity's quest for peace and compassion. Thus, all knowledge students learn is related to the world we want to build in the 21st century.

When we take a new perspective on knowledge, new learning approaches appear. In studying history, we may want to ask this question: Who has the right to send others to wars to kill or be killed if we see each and every human being as a divine soul, and if we are all souls on the quest for meaning in life and in the universe? In learning physics, students are guided to see the fundamental importance of interdependence and interconnectedness that sustains the balance of nature. In language, students learn about the power of language and use it to elevate and empower others. In social sciences, students learn the mutual dependence of all people, the common core values that all people share, such as love, compassion, forgiveness, honesty, while deconstructing stereotypes and misunderstandings.

In this approach to teaching and learning, the class becomes something like an organic particle of the universe, dancing in rhythm with it, living with it; it is small yet it is connected to the hearts and souls of all people and things, to the past, present, and future. We listen to each other's heartbeats and heed our souls' voices. The boundary between ages, between geographical locations, the division based on status, race, class, and gender all break down. Teaching and learning are bonded; classroom and the world are one, and individuals and the collective are united. We do not just interpret the world, we *feel* and *live with* the world. The speaker speaks with the heart, and the listener listens with the soul.

The teacher does not perform the teaching act—the teacher is sharing her life's understanding with students, and vice versa. Teaching is treated as an art of living, with exquisite beauty and incredible responsibility, as the teacher's acts impress and influence the quest of the students' souls.

Teachers then see their accomplishment in terms of molding the soul, shining the light of love into it, and helping to brighten the world and the universe with their love. The teacher is one who has mastered the technical knowledge of the text but more importantly the knowledge of life and the wisdom of the soul, and who integrates them into the holistic act of education.

The kind of teaching I have outlined cannot be accomplished by teachers alone. Collaboration in teaching is essential. Teachers working together can create a synergistic environment that will have a consistent impact on students. Teachers working together also present wonderful opportunities for each other to practice teaching and living with love. Teachers working together enlarge the learning circle.

INSTITUTIONALIZING WISDOM-BASED EDUCATION

Education for love and wisdom opens up the whole being in ourselves and includes the whole world and universe as our object of study. This new paradigm requires institutional support, as education is inextricably linked with the cultural and political systems of our society. We need to reconsider the structure of the school, which institutionalizes care and love so that teachers not only can show intimacy and care for children but are also encouraged and required to do so, and rewarded for it.

A primary responsibility of educators is that they not only be aware of the general conditions that affect the shaping of actual experience, but that they also recognize what concrete surroundings are conducive to having experiences that lead to growth (learning is a process; it is fluid, changing, fun). Above all, they should know how to utilize the surroundings, physical and social, that exist so as to extract from them all that they have to contribute to building experiences that are worthwhile (Dewey 1938, p. 40).

Dewey's words inform us that the total school environment should encourage the search for wisdom. Ways of organizing the curriculum, of scheduling classes, of offering extracurricular activities, of including parents and community—all need to be reconceptualized and built into the very structure of education for wisdom.

LOVE AND WISDOM: INSEPARABLE QUALITIES

Education for wisdom is premised on an education for love. Love as goodness is the foundation of wisdom. Without love there won't be wisdom. Love-based wisdom helps us to rise above separation and see our wholeness. It is inherently an understanding of the deep interconnectedness of our world. Wisdom provides us a vision for what structurally and functionally work for a peaceful, loving, and sustainable world. Education for wisdom is thus education for what makes the world peaceful, loving, and sustainable. Education for wisdom is also related to a deep concern for the direction our society is heading toward. It has to be a striving for a better world.

The deepest kind of love-based wisdom requires what Harry R. Halloran Jr. and Lawrence S. Bale believe; that is, we need to form a new relationship with the global ecosystem, develop a global consciousness, formulate, define, implement and promote a global ethic, and move toward a global society that will be characterized by a newly complexified global consciousness. They call for "interreligious dialogue" that recognizes the plurality of the world's religious systems as a valuable resource for discovering and working together toward common goals. They urge a "stretch of the imagination" to envision the global ecosystem as the embodiment of a holistically emergent global ecomind:

> Consequently, if we are going to successfully meet "the greatest challenge that has confronted the human race in its entire history," and "solve the common problems that threaten our future on the earth," our modes of envisioning a *global ethic*—which will serve as the template for humankind's newly emergent *global ethos*—will have to reflect and cooperate creatively with the knowledge and wisdom evident in the patterns that sustain the *global ecomind*. (Halloran and Bale)

If we as educators have this kind of broad vision in mind, and align our work with pursuing these goals for the benefit of all people and existences, we will be seekers, as well as transmitters, of wisdom.

Chapter Eight

Educational Leadership in the 21st Century

A huge challenge for educational leaders in the 21st century is to visualize the need of our society to learn to coexist in peace and to live in harmony with nature. Leaders with such a vision set new goals and priorities for educators in the rebuilding of our world based on love, forgiveness, respect, and understanding. They are committed to bringing up new generations of people who are equipped with the wisdom, knowledge, skills, and attributes to construct a beloved community in their institutions and in their daily lives.

The visionary educational leaders of the 21st century are those who harbor profound love for humanity and for all existences. Love is an essential quality of any leaders in education, for love fosters understanding and forgiveness, gives birth to true compassion and respect, and enhances cooperation. Love guides lost souls back to the right path and gives our world new hope.

THE PROBLEMS OF CONVENTIONAL LEADERSHIP

Leadership prevailing in our society and school system today still follows the conventional mode. It is still based on a top-down structure, founded on a division between "us" and "others."

We thus need a great transformation of leadership, one that can facilitate deep dialogues among cultures and people, one that can bridge misunderstandings and bring people together to work for peace and harmony in our world. Leaders who will take us to such a new future will be leaders of peace, who will lead not with coercion but with unconditional love and forgiveness.

Conventional leadership cannot equip humanity with the tools to deal with the many crises we are facing today. The new leadership I envision is not defined in terms of power and authority, but in terms of the leaders' ability to exemplify unconditional, universal love and care, with leaders serving as the living role models of forgiveness and compassion for *all*. It is encouraging to see that in recent decades a momentum has gathered for introducing new and alternative modes of leadership, such as caring leadership, servant leadership, and transformational leadership, which aim at breaking down all barriers that lead to separation and hatred, and that unite us to begin building a new world where we no longer inflict pain on each other.

Conventional leadership focuses on wielding power to coerce people to take directions they do not want to take. Countries are dragged into wars even though a large number of their citizens protest the leadership's policy. Citizens often are deprived of their voices and cannot exercise their critical, moral, and spiritual intelligence at times of crisis. A hierarchical structure in most of our societies allows officials to cling to power and reap personal benefits, taking advantage of their public office. Conventional leadership is furthermore based on the notion of separation between human beings and nature, and separation between human beings. Labeling and categorizing of others as enemies, and countries and parties condemning each other in antagonistic terms, are daily happenings. The current nation-state structure allows leaders to mobilize the masses and resources of a whole nation, in some cases resources of multiple nations, to engage in wars and destroy each other for "justice."

Conventional leadership has led us nowhere in the past 2000 years but has plunged us into wars and chaos; it is now taking us closer than ever to the point of total destruction. It is high time that leaders unequivocally and unconditionally renounce all wars and focus on solving our problems through universal love, forgiveness, and reconciliation. We need authentic leaders who know human oneness deeply, who find it inconceivable to inflict pain and suffering on our brothers and sisters and on Mother Nature. The new leadership must steadfastly focus on the goals of peace and harmony, to give *all* human beings and existences the rights and dignity to live. The Earth, richly bestowed by Mother Nature, has enough resources to feed all human beings, to keep all of us warm, and to provide opportunities for all of us to receive a high quality education that facilitates our development spiritually, morally, emotionally, and intellectually. Mother Nature also has enough to take care of all animals and other species. The condition is that we see others' well-being as our own, and that we take actions to build a truly equal, all-inclusive, compassionate society for all.

THE NEW LEADERSHIP CRITERIA

The universe is a unity. All humanities and all existences are linked in soul, spirit, energy, and material existence through a vast field of energy. . Through this boundless field of energy, our well-being and soul development, our thoughts, deeds, and words are inextricably connected, and the distribution of energy is based on the principle of "virtue as the essence" (Yan 1996d, 1997). Those who are practicing loving leadership have the power to work with this immense field of energy, as their work benefits a large number of people and their influence spreads out like the wave in a pond, vibrating out to a larger and larger circle.

Water flows from high to low, and energy does the same. When we are able to treat each other with respect and humility, we are abundantly rewarded by an incessant flow of energy, which comes as support from people. In Eastern philosophy, our length of life has everything to do with the accumulation of energy through virtuous acts. "The virtuous live a long life" is a Chinese saying. Wisdom from Chinese traditional philosophy also posits that a country focusing on virtue will last long and become prosperous. Arrogance will bring an outflow of energy and a departure of support. Hence, wise leaders are those who store up good will, lend help wherever there is a need, and in time of crisis help their people effectively by getting the support of other people and other countries.

Great leaders in human history have a common virtue: They do not work for themselves; they do not seek the fruits of their action in power and fame; they have no fear of losing wealth and fame, for they are not attached to them. They see right into the soul—they see the beauty of creation in each and every individual and in each and every existence. They acutely sense the joy and pain of all people. In their eyes, there are no "bad people" or "enemies," but only those who need help and support. These people can be religious leaders, spiritual teachers, accomplished professionals, or political leaders, but most of them are ordinary people who are loved by many but who do not have a wide reputation because of their indifference to fame.

In sum, the challenge in the 21st century is to create alternative theories and priorities for leadership development. Not only do we need leaders with vision, we also need to ask these questions when we select leaders: Is the vision laid out by the leaders going to lead us to the building of an equal society? Are their policies helping us form a new global community that allows for true respect and understanding? Are the leaders using their office to have power over people or to do service for people? Further, we need to reexamine what qualities we are seeking in leaders. Is intellectual ability enough? What are the leader's combined qualities in terms of emotional, moral, ecological, and spiritual intelligence? Ultimately, are they loving leaders?

NEW EDUCATIONAL LEADERSHIP

In this light, new leadership in the education of the 21st century should focus first and foremost on the enlightened understanding that we are all equal spirits, and that this core essence transcends our external differences such as race, class, gender, nationality, and so forth. The leaders are hence tender-hearted human beings who feel the pain and joy of the human soul and Mother Nature. They have an abundance of compassion, care, love, understanding, respect, and forgiveness to offer to children and teachers. In these leaders' hearts, the joy and pain of the whole school community are felt and understood deeply and experientially. These feelings are translated into an administrative style of loving kindness toward all children and teachers in their schools, thus transforming their schools into schools for love.

In the 21st century, in order to change the perception of separation of ourselves from others, which enables political and military leadership to justify killings and suffering with various excuses, we are ripe for the advent of educative leaders who set a high priority on healing emotional and spiritual wounds, on bridging gaps in global and local cultural understanding. In their eyes there are no enemies, only people who need help or understanding. Educative leaders are committed to nonviolence. They resort to the power of love, service, respect, humility, understanding, trust, and honesty as powerful tools for changing the new generation into a force of peace. They enable the younger generation to see that we cannot overcome evil by adding more and more weapons of mass destruction. They aim at transforming students to become visionary peace workers who take the long-term survival of humankind and Mother Nature to heart, and take actions in a responsible manner for the common good. They seek no fame for themselves; they bear no anger or hatred toward anyone. Their hearts are filled with boundless love and unconditional acceptance; they see only brothers and sisters on earth, not separated, alienated individual beings who are opponents. They enlighten students through the example of service and love, showing students that this is the way to maintain peace and harmony.

Courage and Big Heart

Obviously, the new leadership requires a new set of world views, and takes a new way of knowing. Especially, the new leadership requires great courage to embrace and live the new views. In other words, the new leadership requires a courageous display of unconditional love and forgiveness, despite the harsh realities and misunderstanding in our current world situation. It is this courage that rallies people around the leaders to rise above hatred and vengeance, and to bring victims and victimizers together as brothers and sisters to resolve their problems.

It also takes great courage for the educative leaders to communicate a sense of urgency for us to break down all walls and barriers among people for a global, harmonious family. They urge the new generation to go beyond all the superficial differences among people, be they gender, class, ethnicity, religion, or nationality, and see our true value as equal spirits and souls. They ask students not only to wish God to bless "our people," "our nation," but they wish for the good of all human beings and for all existences on Earth. Memories of pain are preserved not for revenge, but for reminding us how much we need to learn to love, and what we need to do consistently to make the world a better place.

Teachers as Leaders

In the 21st century, the notion of leaders should be vastly expanded. Those people who work with the souls and hearts of people, whose job involves a lot of love, care, understanding, and service, are leaders of a new era. In this sense, teachers are our future leaders for constructing a new world through their work with the heart and mind. Teachers are leaders who exemplify to our young people what love, care, compassion, respect, and understanding are. In teaching and curriculum practice, teachers are frontline leaders who empower students to acquire knowledge and wisdom to change our society for the common good. Teachers are leaders who demonstrate to our young people commitment for service and giving. Teachers as leaders tell students that in order to lead one must be a servant first, and students learn from the role modeling of teachers to become responsible, global, and peace-making citizens.

We are living in an open and global world. Future teacher-leaders must adopt an open mind and an interconnected view of their role in the world. Open-minded teacher-leaders see themselves as training global citizens who must learn to respect each other and live in harmony. Teacher-leaders know that a better world will be built upon the power of love, not the power of weapons. They see that the clash of cultures must be transformed into a dialogue among people, and we must develop a true appreciation of the beauty of the world's cultures.

Service Leadership

Eugene Habecker says,

> The true leader serves. Serves people. Serves their best interests, and in so doing will not always be popular, may not always impress. But because true leaders are motivated by loving concern rather than a desire for personal glory, they are willing to pay the price. (quoted in Maxwell 1999, p. 133)

Today, scholars and the general public alike are advocating service leadership. Service leadership is about getting people to form inclusive, supportive, and empowering relationships; the leaders' responsibilities are to motivate and support people to accomplish change or make a difference to benefit the common good. The leaders are committed to their followers; they are a "repository" of shared leadership, as "the leader no longer acts on followers but is engaged in action with followers who are acting with the leader" (Drath 2001, p. 70). The leaders empower, inspire, and motivate others to do their best. They lead from their heart, and they see powers not as theirs but as the precious opportunity to serve others. They have a keen eye for how their service impacts the future. For them, their achievement is measured by the enlargement of others, the growth and success of others.

Leaders for Love

Many scholars and leaders have pinpointed that the needed qualities for a leader are that they have passion, they listen, they care, and they are willing to go the extra mile to take responsibility. Yet the greatest leaders of human history have been leaders who demonstrate the highest kind of virtue: unconditional love. Gandhi and King are two contemporaries. They are leaders for love.

Leaders for love can be teachers or administrators. They should empower students to learn love from the living experience of their lives. They need to create an atmosphere where students feel appreciative of the love they have received from parents, friends, teachers, and yes, strangers. Students need to know it is because of many people's work that we are able to have food on the table and keep warm during cold winters. We have received so much before we have given to society. Through a new lens, a lens of love, they see how much they have been blessed by other people's love.

Leaders for love should encourage students to use love as a lens to gain a heightened sense of justice to feel strongly for the suffering of people in the world and hence cultivate great compassion for all. Leaders should see that love and respect are the source of strength, the source of wisdom, that success in life is inextricably bound with virtues of love, care, respect, understanding, and forgiveness. Through the lens of love, all boundaries break down. We are not divided by race, class, gender, national borders, and so on; rather, we are bound and integrated by love.

Leaders for love should guide students and teachers to explore deep down the most earnest desires of our hearts: acceptance, respect, love, joy, and giving. Leaders for love use their hearts to listen to their teachers and students. They have unshakeable faith that young people will become loving residents of Earth. They see their students in a positive light, learn from them, guide them, encourage them, and appreciate them for who they are. They encourage students to explore questions about nature, life, love, virtue, the universe, and so on. They have a broad vision of where students can learn, how students can learn, and what students can learn, so that they take life as an exploration and expansion for students, and their classroom can hold all of humanity and the whole universe in it! The commitment of the leader is demonstrated in their unwavering belief in the power of love for a better future.

Ultimately, with leaders for love, we will train our future generations to totally reject the building of weapons of mass destruction; we will not allow any elected officials to wage wars and justify killing through various excuses. We will have citizens that never obey orders to kill—for all those called "others" are seen as part of ourselves, and killing others is equal to killing ourselves. Future citizens will not only have minds to think, but also hearts full of love and compassion to feel and experience. It is leaders for love who light up the road and lead the people onto the path of eternal peace and harmony with nature.

WOMEN AND LEADERSHIP

Women must assume important roles in leadership. Women's voices have been marginalized, and women have been excluded from important positions in government and in all sectors of our society. Patriarchal systems define love, care, compassion, empathy, and connection as feminine traits and give them low value. The unequal economic structure we have built up in our society has created a jungle mentality based on predatory values. If we adopt new standards and values regarding leadership in the 21st century, as I have outlined throughout this book, women will have a much bigger role to play in local and global leadership. Not only women, but both women and men who show qualities of love, compassion, service, understanding, and forgiveness need to be in leadership positions to take us in a new direction.

Women are not any less capable than men of helping to improve our current situation and bring about global peace, of curing each other and nature.

In fact, women may have an advantage, being more caring and intuitive and spiritual overall. If at least half of all leadership positions are filled by women, we will have a new world. It is conceivable that in two or three decades, as many women as men will be in leadership positions, as we begin to wake up to the power of love to save ourselves and live in harmony and peace.

TWENTY-FIRST-CENTURY LEADERSHIP: A NEW FORM ON THE HORIZON

We must redefine the notion of leadership. The traditional notion of leadership that emphasizes the grabbing of power and fame is outdated. If we are to build a society for love, we need to change many of our criteria: For example, leadership should be willingness to support, to sacrifice, to treat all human beings and all existences with great compassion, to forgive and to heal. We will adjust to this perspective that leadership is about exalting others, helping the disadvantaged, giving without thinking about return, treating all people and all existences with deep love and respect. Leadership will be about humility and compassion, about nurturing the heart and spirit of people.

In the 21st century, we will have hope when we have leaders who treat each and every human being as a divine soul; who treat animals, plants, mountains, rivers, and oceans as divine souls; who have a very deep understanding of the reciprocity of life and energy. The leaders will suffer before others, and claim credit behind others; they will give glory and fame to others and be willing to remain unfamous. They will seek no material possessions and will see themselves as being rich in the pursuit of spiritual, moral, and transcendental development. We need leaders who unconditionally search for only constructive solutions to all problems, who can heal pain and cleanse people's hearts of bitterness and despair with unconditional love. This is the leadership of hope for the 21st century.

THE FUTURE OF HUMANKIND: IT STARTS WITH OUR ACTS NOW

If we truly feel the suffering of others with our heart and heed the crying of souls, we will have less difficulty supporting all efforts that have been made by millions of people for building peace, for providing universal healthcare, for giving quality education to all, for supporting international and domestic efforts to protect our environment and all creatures living on Earth. We will see clearly that channeling huge amounts of financial and material resources into the building of weapons is wrong and insane, that allowing some people to be overwhelmingly rich while millions are starving is wrong and unjust. We will not allow major decisions to be made for us, rather we will all be decision makers for peace.

It takes tremendous courage for leaders to shift from a positivistic, efficiency, capitalist model to one that emphasizes the centrality of education for love, that sees a child as a full human being whose life purpose is to learn to give love and receive love. It takes courage to act on one's belief; and it takes courage to have a vision, a vision for a new form of curriculum, a new school culture, a new form of teacher-student relationship, and a new set of outcomes for our students through education.

Leaders of courage do not shy away from talking about values. They embody the values they are trying to impart in their daily acts of management. They are loving, caring, fair, honest, respectful, and helpful. They do not stress their own authority or power, rather they empower their teachers and students to be greater than they are, to fulfill their greatest potential.

The new leaders must be willing to perform reconciliatory leadership, caring leadership, service leadership, sharing leadership, compassionate leadership, equality leadership, moral leadership, and spiritual leadership. They use the power of love from their hearts and souls to rally people for a future of long-lasting peace and harmony. They unite people in a solid brotherhood and sisterhood where everyone treats others just they would treat themselves and their own family members. The world is one that is for the good for all, and everyone works for the good of all.

Chapter Nine

School for Love, World for Love

We need a powerful vision for a new world. A vision centered on the power of love will empower us to create a new world. Love for all people and existences is the underlying global ethic that will unite us to work for a peaceful, ecologically sustainable future. Schools for love nurture future global citizens to become persons who care deeply, who integrate compassion and love into every facet of their lives; eventually, this kind of education will transform the social, political, and economic structures of our society. A school for love breeds a society for love, and vice versa. Hence, school and society need to work together for our dream to come true.

School for love is about nurturing a loving member in a family, a community, a company, a school, and a society; it is about nurturing a loving relationship between humankind and nature. Based on the principle of love, we foster compassion, respect, forgiveness, and understanding; and from universal love springs a profound sense of social and ecological responsibility, and actions to correct past wrongs and usher in a better future.

Teaching love is the sacred task not only of future schools, it is also for family, community, society, and the world as a whole. School and society constantly influence each other to create a culture for love, a culture of peace, and a culture for the coexistence of all creatures on Earth.

FAMILY FOR LOVE

Family is the foundational unit in society. A loving family is the foundation of a loving school. When students know what it is to be loved and cared for in the family, they will be more ready to show these qualities toward fellow students in school.

Thus, knowing love in one's family is the first step to learning trust to others and learning about caring and reciprocal concern. If students cannot learn to love their parents, who give them life and nurture them, it is hard to ask them to extend their love to others in the larger world. Parents are thus the most important teachers in children's lives.

Parents are the first teachers of their children. If they want to cultivate their children's IQ, they must themselves love learning; if they want their children to have high EQ and MQ, they must model concern and respect for others and display compassion and forgiveness for all. They must be available to guide their children throughout the process of forming values and habits based on a universal love for all humanity and nature. Family is the best place to form values that are conducive to the building of a wonderful world, for family is a small world in itself. Hence, as parents, when we think of our children's education we ought to see our role as teachers, role models, and students as well. Parents lay the foundation for what their children will become. If parents have a vision of a loving world in mind all the time, they will consciously create an environment for children to cultivate strong beliefs in the power of love and help schools tremendously in becoming places for love.

FROM A LOVING FAMILY TO A LOVING COMMUNITY

Most of us know how much our parents love and care for us. In fact, love is a commonality among most family members. However, it takes many loving families to form a loving community.

For many people, it is difficult to extend one's love outside one's family toward outsiders or strangers. We have been scared by reports in the media and stories in daily life into distrusting people whom we do not know; we take selfishness as basic in others and thus see only the family as the place we may find true love and trust.

A loving community requires that we reach out and care for the well-being of neighbors and local organizations, such as schools and hospitals. A loving community gives people opportunities to learn to care for each other, to help those who are sick, and to provide support for those in need of emotional and spiritual help. These communities can take the form of a book club, an NGO, a professional organization, a church, a group of friends, or a mentoring group for young people. Regardless of members' professions and status, they are all members of the loving communities wherein everyone is treated as a beloved group member.

A loving community ensures a continuity in what the students learn at home and school. When students join these communities, they continue to learn and practice the power of love by giving, sharing, helping, forgiving, reconciling, and communicating. The communities provide them with an environment in which they can become contributing members to society.

FROM A LOVING COMMUNITY TO A LOVING SOCIETY

Our society has been stratified by race, class, gender, and many factors irrelevant to our true essence as equal souls and spirits. Poverty has been sustained by a division of people based on their possessions and status. It takes the vision of a loving society to overcome inequality among people and move on to a world for all.

Creating a loving society requires members of the society to fundamentally analyze where things have gone wrong and work collectively to address those issues. This may call for drastic change in laws, social organizations, and structures; we may have to overhaul political and economic leadership, the role of the mass media, and so on. At this point it seems difficult to do this, but we need to begin imagining and awaken ourselves to this urgency. In my Education for Global Peace class, I ask the students to imagine what they could do to bring peace. It is amazing to hear how many creative solutions we have. Some propose hiring retired Red Cross workers and development workers to mentor young people on conflict resolution; one student suggested using half of the United States' military budget to send American citizens abroad to build cultural bridges and respect; one student outlined in great detail how peace education could be fully integrated into the policy and curriculum of a state education system; and another student gave a whole new notion about how we can organize our society: How about a Department of Peace rather than a Defense Department, a Department of Economic Equality and Justice rather than a Department of Commerce, and a Department of Cultural Bridge-Building rather than the State Department? With this kind of imagination and determination for peace, we can some day eliminate all violence from the society. Impossible solutions today become possible when, as a collective force, we decide that this is what makes our society work, and work better.

We need to have the courage and creativity to imagine what works for our future. All of these hinge on our realizing our oneness as a human race and as one element of nature and the universe.

FROM A LOVING SOCIETY TO A LOVING WORLD

We are living in a shrinking world. Yet national borders are still preventing us from seeing each other as global loving family members. Cultural differences are still creating big misunderstandings. Religious groups are claiming their "truth" as the ultimate truth while rejecting the validity of others.

Technological development and the information highway have pointed us to a future where national boundaries may break down and a global consciousness is born. Globalization, even with its negative consequences, is ushering in a global interdependent economy and interdependent society. This information and economic interconnectedness, however, are insufficient. We need to build bridges that connect the hearts and souls of people, and only an ethos of universal love can accomplish this. Hence, a loving world needs to be one that no longer places one country's national interests above those of others; a loving world is built with each country reaching out wherever people are still suffering from poverty and natural disasters. Loving schools, families, communities, and societies bind us in a loving world.

FROM A LOVING WORLD TO A LOVING UNIVERSE

A loving world needs to have a loving relationship with nature, with all that exists in the universe. Without deep respect for the universe, we may be ruining not only ourselves but also bringing danger to the universe. The solar system, for example, needs the healthy existence of the Earth; the imbalance of the Earth's ecosystem may bring imbalance to the solar system, which may bring about major changes in other planetary systems as well. Thus, we need a view of the universe that links our planet's well-being to that of the whole universe.

LOVE AS THE HOPE OF OUR ULTIMATE FREEDOM

Love is the ultimate hope for freedom from wars, suffering, separation, social inequality, and environmental devastation. In order to construct a consensus, we need to have a turnaround in our thinking, to see love as our survival strategy, our solution to social problems, and our contribution and obligation to the world and the universe. We need to nurture love as critically important for our functioning as individuals, as a family, as a society, and as a world.

CONCLUSION

Family, school, and society are one unity. For the school for love to fly, families and communities must be places where children learn love and compassion firsthand. A good family relies on parents having received a loving education; a good school relies on children having learned love from a loving family; a loving society relies on generations of people having received loving education. A positive cycle is formed when family, school, and society work together.

A good school is like a good family. It gives students a sense of belonging. It allows children to feel love and trust, and to be themselves. Teachers treat their students like their own children, and students treat their teachers like their parents—because there is love.

Bertrand Russell (1967) states of his life,

> Three passions, simply but overwhelmingly strong, have governed my life: The longing for love, the search for knowledge and unbearable pity of the suffering of mankind.

As individuals and as a human race, we should all pursue these three passions. Love leads to the second passion, which is wisdom-knowledge, and from love arises the oneness of all.

A paradigm shift takes courage, as breaking away from the old paradigm is breaking away from the old self, the old thought pattern. There will be such strong resistance in ourselves and in the external environment that many will be scared at the beginning. As Kuhn (1996) says,

> The source of the resistance is the assurance that the older paradigm will ultimately solve its problems, that nature can be shoved into the box the paradigm provides. . . . A generation is sometimes required to effect the change. (pp. 151–152)

In order to give birth to a new paradigm based on love, we need to persist and work as a whole. We must be the momentum builder and believe that once the streams merge together, the torrent of change will be unstoppable.

When enough people change the way they view things, then solutions become evident, often in ways we couldn't even imagine before we looked with new eyes (Hartmann 1999, p. 3).

Only love can transform the heart. The solidarity of humanity can be built only upon love. Only love can transcend our differences and connect all people and all existences as a unified family. Based on love, we need to cultivate total forgiveness, total understanding, and total respect. It is only through this that we as a human race can stop violence.

There are deep-seated forces in the cosmos creating, nurturing, and pre-serving life. It is the all-pervasive love that flows in the universe that enables life to come into being and to be. Love is the energy of the universe. To love is to be in tandem with the energy of the universe.

As Gandhi says, love and truth are two sides of a coin. When one has true knowledge, one has love. When one embraces love, one arrives at truth.

Let's embrace truth!

Bibliography

Alexander, Hanan. (2001). *Reclaiming Goodness: Education and the Spirtual Quest*. Notre Dame, IN: University of Notre Dame Press.

Ayres, Alex, ed. (1993). *The Wisdom of Martin Luther King, Jr*. New York: Meridian.

Belenky, Mary F., Blythe Clinchy, Nancy Rule Goldberger, and Jill Mattuck Tarule. (1986). *Women's Ways of Knowing: The Development of Self, Voice, and Mind*. New York: Basic Books.

Berry, Thomas. (1988). *The Dream of the Earth*. San Francisco: Sierra Club Books.

Bey, Theresa, and Gwendolyn Turner. (1996). *Making School a Place of Peace*. California: Corwin Press.

Bohm, David. (1980). *Wholeness and the Implicate Order*. London: Routledge.

Borba, Michele. (2001). *Building Moral Intelligence: The Seven Essential Virtues that Teach Kids to Do the Right Thing*. San Francisco: Jossey-Bass.

Boulding, Elise. (2000). *Cultures of Peace: The Hidden Side of History*. Syracuse, NY: Syracuse University Press.

Cajete, Gregory. (1999). "The making of an indigenous teacher: Insights into the ecology of teaching." In Jeffrey Kane, ed., *Education, Information and Transformation: Essays on Learning and Thinking*. Upper Saddle River, NJ: Merrill.

Capra, Fritjof. (1999). *The Tao of Physics* (5th ed.). Boston: Shambhala.

Carson, Clayborne, and Peter Holloran, eds. (1998). *A Knock at Midnight: Inspiration from the Great Sermons of Reverend Martin Luther King, Jr*. New York: IPM/Warner Books.

Chopra, Deepak. (1990). *Quantum Healing: Exploring the Frontiers of Mind/Body Medicine*. New York: Bantam Books.

Chopra, Deepak. (1998). *Ageless Body, Timeless Mind: The Quantum Alternative to Growing Old*. New York: Three Rivers Press.

Coles, Robert. (1997). *The Moral Intelligence of Children*. New York: Random House.

Conze, Edward. (2001). *Buddhist Wisdom: The Diamond Sutra and Heart Sutra*. New York: Vintage Books.

Delpit, Lisa D. (1995). *Other People's Children: Cultural Conflict in the Classroom*. New York: New Press.

Dewey, John. (1938). *Experience and Education*. New York: MacMillan.

Dossey, Larry. (1993). *Healing Words: The Power of Prayer and the Practice of Medicine*. New York: Harper.

Drath, Wilfred. (2001). *The Deep Blue Sea: Rethinking the Source of Leadership*. San Francisco: Jossey-Bass.

Eadie, Betty J. (1992). *Embraced by the Light*. New York: Bantam Books.

Eco, Umberto. (1997). *The Search for the Perfect Language*. Oxford: Blackwell.

Emmons, Robert A. (1999). *The Psychology of Ultimate Concern: Motivation and Spirituality in Personality*. New York: Guilford.

Finley, Laura. (2003). "How can I teach peace when the book only covers war?" *OJPCR: The Online Journal of Peace and Conflict Resolution* 5, no.1 (Summer): 150–165. www.trinstitute.org/ojpcr/5_1finley.htm.

Freire, Paulo. (2000). *Pedagogy of the Oppressed*. New York: Continuum.

Gandhi, Mohandas K., ed. (1999). *The Way to God*. Berkeley, CA: Berkeley Hills.

Gardner, Howard. (1993). *Multiple Intelligences: Theory in Practice*. New York: Basic Books.

Gardner, Howard. (1999). *Intelligence Reframed*. New York: Basic Books.

Goldstein, Lisa S. (1998). *Teaching with Love: A Feminist Approach to Early Childhood Education*. New York: Peter Lang.

Goleman, Daniel. (1995). *Emotional Intelligence*. New York: Bantam Books.

Goleman, Daniel. (1998). *Working with Emotional Intelligence*. New York: Bantam Books.

Goodman, Jeffrey. (1979). *We Are the Earthquake Generation*. New York: Berkeley Publishing Corporation.

Greene, Maxine. (1993). "Diversity and inclusion: Toward a curriculum for human beings." *Teachers College Record* 95, no. 2: pp. 211–221.

Halloran, Harry R., Jr., and Lawrence S. Bale. "Toward a viable global ethos." http://astro.temple.edu/~dialogue/lsb_an.htm.

Harris, Ian, and Mary Lee Morrison. (2003). *Peace Education*. New York: Mcfarland & Co.

Hartmann, Thom. (1999). *The Last Hours of Ancient Sunlight: Waking Up to Personal and Global Transformation*. New York: Three Rivers Press.

Helman, Herbert C., and V. Lee Hamilton. (1989). *Crime of Obedience*. New Haven, CT: Yale University Press.

Hicks, David, ed. (1988) *Education for Peace: Issues, Principles, and Practice in the Classroom*. London: Routledge.

hooks, bell. (1994). *Teaching to Transgress: Education as the Practice of Freedom*. New York: Routledge.

Hunt, Valerie V. (1996). *Infinite Mind: Science of the Human Vibrations of Consciousness*. Malibu, CA: Malibu.

Huntington, Samuel. (1996). *The Clash of Civilizations and the Remaking of World Order*. New York: Touchstone.

Hutchison, David. (1998). *Growing up Green: Education for Ecological Renewal*. New York: Teachers College.

Illich, Ivan. (2000). *Deschooling Society*. St. Paul, MN: Marion Boyars Publishers.

International Yan Xin Qigong Association. (1997). *Yan Xin Qigong Collectanea*, vols. 1–9. New York: International Yan Xin Qigong Scientific Association.

Jain, Devaki. (2000). Healing the wounds of development. In Jill K. Conway and Susan C. Bourque, eds., *The Politics of Women's Education*. Ann Arbor: University of Michigan Press, pp. 45–58.

Jing Wei, and Ai, Ren, eds. (1998). *Philosophy and Practice of Yan Xin Qigong*. Shenzhen: Haitian Publishing House.

Kafato, Menas, and Robert Nadea. (2000). *The Conscious Universe*. New York: Springer-Verlag.

Kalb, Claudia. (2003). Faith and Healing. *Newsweek* (November 10): pp. 44–56.

Kessler, Rachael. (2000). *The Soul of Education*. Alexandria, VA: Association for Supervision and Curriculum Development.

King, Martin Luther, Jr. (1957). *Loving Your Enemies*. http://www.mlkonline.net/enemies.html.

King, Martin Luther, Jr. (1963a). *Strength to Love*. New York: Harper & Row, p. 133.

King, Martin Luther, Jr. (1963b). "I Have a Dream." Speech delivered at the Lincoln Memorial. Washington D.C. (August 28).

King, Martin Luther, Jr. (1964). Nobel Prize acceptance speech. Stockholm (December 11).

King, Martin Luther, Jr. (1967a). *Beyond Vietnam: A Time to Break Silence*. http://www.blackcommentator.com/25/25_king.html.

King, Martin Luther, Jr. (1967b). *The Trumpet of Conscience*. New York: Harper & Row.

Kizza, Joseph, M. (1998). *Civilizing the Internet: Global Concerns and Efforts toward Regulation*. Jefferson, NC: MaFarland.

Kripalani, Krishna. (2001). *Gandhi: All Men are Brothers*. New York: Continuum.

Krippner, Stanley, and Daniel Rubin. (1973). *Galaxies of Life: The Human Aura in Acupuncture and Kirlian Photography*. New York: Gordon and Breach, Science Publishers.

Kuhn, Thomas S. (1996). *The Structure of Scientific Revolutions*. Chicago: University of Chicago Press.

Kung, Hans. (1991). *Global Responsibility: In Search of a New World Ethic*. New York: Crossroad.

Lantieri, Linda, and Janet Patti. (1996). *Waging Peace in Our Schools*. Boston: Beacon Press.

Lao Zi. *Dao De Jing*. In *Tian Chengyang* (ed). Classics of Taoism (Daojin zhishi baodian). Sichuan, China: Sichuan People's Publishing House, pp. 150–168.

Lasley, Thomas J., II. (1994). *Teaching Peace: Toward Cultural Selflessness*. Westport, CT: Bergin and Garvey.

Lee, Chung Ok. (2000). "Triple universal ethics for a new civilization." In Chung Ok Lee, ed., *Vision for a New Civilization: Spiritual and Ethical Values in the New Millennium*. New York: Won Buddhism Publishing, pp. 161–199.

Lin, Jing. (2005). "Building Bridges, Working for a Better World." In *"Strangers" of the Academy: Asian Female Scholars in Higher Education*. Sterling, VA: Stylus Publishing. In press.

Lin, Jing, and Heidi Ross. (2004a). "Environmental education in China: Policy, theory, and prospects." *Chinese Education and Society* (August/September).

Lin, Jing, and Heidi Ross. (2004b). "Environmental education in China: Green schools and practices." *Chinese Education and Society* (May/June).

Lin, Jing. (1991). *The Red Guards' Path to Violence*. New York: Praeger.

Lippman, Thomas. (1995). *Understanding Islam: An Introduction to the Muslim World*. New York: Meridian.

Maxwell, John C. (1999). *The 21 Indispensable Qualities of a Leader*. Nashville, TN: Thomas Nelson.

Milbrath, Lester W. (1996). *Learning to Think Environmentally: While There is Still Time*. Albany: State University of New York Press.

Miller, John P., and Yoshiharu Makagawa. (2002). *Nurturing Our Wholeness: Perspective on Spirituality in Education*. Brandon, VT: Foundation for Educational Renewal.

Miller, John P. (1994). *The Contemplative Practitioner: Meditation in Education and the Professions*. Toronto: OISE Press.

Mische, Patricia M. (2000). "A more humane world order: Towards a new civilization." In Chung Ok Lee, ed., *Vision for a New Civilization: Spiritual and Ethical Values in the New Millennium*. New York: Won Buddhism Publishing, pp. 117–160.

Mitchell, Stephen, trans. (2000). *Bhagavad Gita*. New York: Harmony Books.

Myers, David G. (2000). *The American Paradox: Spiritual Hunger in an Age of Plenty*. New Haven, CT: Yale University Press.

Nava, Ramon Gallegos. (2001). *Holistic Education: Pedagogy of Universal Love*. Bandon, VT: Foundation for Educational Renewal.

Noble, Kathleen D. (2001). *Riding the Windhorse: Spiritual Intelligence and the Growth of the Self*. Cresskill, NJ: Hampton Press.

Noddings, Nel. (1992). *The Challenge to Care in Schools*. New York: Teachers College Press.

Ozmon, Howard, and Samuel Craver. (1999). *Philosophical Foundations of Education* (6th ed.). Columbus, OH: Merrill.

Palmer, Parker J. (1993). *To Know as We Are Known: Education as a Spiritual Journey*. San Francisco: Harper.

Palmer, Parker J. (1998). *The Courage to Teach: Exploring the Inner Landscape of a Teacher's Life*. San Francisco: Jossey-Bass.

Plant, Judith. (1989). *Healing the Wounds: The Promise of Ecofeminism*. Santa Cruz, CA: New Society Publishers.

Plato. (1986). *The symposium*. Middlesex, England: Penguin Books.

Powers, Gerard F., Drew Christiansen, and Robert T. Hennemeyer, eds. (1994). *Peacemaking: Moral and Policy Challenges for a New World*. Washington, D.C.: United States Catholic Conference, Inc.

"Promise." Aired on public TV, November, 2001.

Reagan, Timothy. (2000). *Non-Western Educational Tradition: Alternative Approaches to Educational Thought and Practice*. Mahwah, NJ: Lawrence Erlbawn.

Reardon, Betty A. (1988). *Comprehensive Peace Education: Educating for Global Responsibility*. New York: Teachers College.

Redfield, James. (1997). *The Celestine Vision: Living the New Spiritual Awareness*. New York: Warner Books.

Ruddick, Sara. (1995). *Maternal Thinking: Toward a Politics of Peace*. Boston: Beacon Press.

Russell, Bertrand. (1967). Prologue for *What I Have Lived For*. Cited in Maher, John and Judy Groves. (1996). *Chomsky for Beginners*. London: Icon Books.

Schonberger, Martin. (1992). *The I Ching and the Genetic Code*. Santa Fe, NM: Aurora Press.

Sergiovanni, Thomas J. (1992). *Moral Leadership: Getting to the Heart of School Improvement*. San Francisco: Jossey-Bass.

Smith, David, and Terence R. Carson. (1998). *Education for a Peaceful Future*. Toronto: Kagan and Woo.

Smith, David C. (1999). "De-Militarizing Language." In Bohdan Suchewycz and Jeannette Sloniowski, eds., *Canadian Communications: Issues in Contemporary Media and Culture*. Scarborough, Ontario: Allyn & Bacon, pp. 23–26.

Stern, Paul C. (1992). *Global Environmental Change: Understanding the Human Dimensions*. Washington, D.C.: National Academy Press.

Thompson, J. Milburn. (2000). *Justice and Peace: A Christian Primer*. New York: Orbis Books.

Tompkins, Peter, and Christopher Bird. (1989). *The Secret Life of Plants*. New York: Harper & Row.

Tompkins, Peter, and Christopher Bird (1989). *Secrets of the Soil: New Solutions for Restoring Our Planet*. New York: Harper & Row.

Tong, Rosemarie. (1998). *Feminist Thought: A Comprehensive Introduction*. Boulder, CO: Westview.

Tutu, Desmond. (1999). *No Future without Forgiveness*. New York: Doubleday.

Tutu, Desmond. (2004). *God Has a Dream*. New York: Doubleday.

Walsh, Neale D. (1995). *Conversations with God: An Uncommon Dialogue —Book 1*. New York: G. P. Putnam's Sons.

Walsh, Neale D. (1998). *Conversations with God: An Uncommon Dialogue—Book 3*. Charlottsville, VA: Hampton Roads.

Walsh, Roger. (1999). *Essential Spirituality*. New York: John Wiley & Sons.

Wang Bin. (2001). *The Light of Wisdom: A Reader on Chinese and Western Philosophical Classics*. Shanghai: People's Publisher.

Washington, James M., ed. (1986). *The Essential Writings and Speeches of Martin Luther King, Jr*. San Francisco: Harper San Francisco.

Wyden, Peter, ed. (1984). *Day One before Hiroshima and After*. New York: Simon & Schuster.

Xiaowei, Gong. (1997). *The Book of Piety: The Highest Principle in Human Morality*. Shanghai: Shanghai Classics Publishers.

Xinhua, Wang. (1998). *Basic Theories of Chinese Medicine*. Beijing, China: People's Public Health Publishing House.

Yan Xin. (1996a). *Contribution and Reward*. Toronto: Barbican Publishing.

Yan Xin. (1996b). *The Meaning of Qigong*. Toronto: Barbican Publishing.

Yan Xin. (1996c). *Thought of Qi*. Toronto: Barbican Publishing.

Yan Xin. (1996d). *Virtue is the Essence*. Toronto: Barbican Publishing.

Index

standardization, xvii, 85
stereotypes, 2, 32, 94
Stern, Paul, 71
success, x–xi, 2, 19, 21, 23–24, 35, 42,
44, 51, 76–77, 83, 86, 100;
redefining, 35
survival, ix, xii, xiv, xvii, 5, 8, 9, 11–12,
50, 64, 72, 74, 81–82; collective, 14,
26; environmental, 37, 71, 83; of the
fittest, 22; of humankind, 98;
physical, 20; and prosperity, 8, 92;
strategy, 108; and sustainability, 5,
71, 86; of our whole civilization, 82
sustainability, 50, 70–72, 75, 83, 86, 91
synchronicity, 75

Tao (or the Way), 44, 63, 65, 75, 80 82,
88
Taoism, 17, 44, 47, 55, 75, 82
teacher training, 90
teacher-student relationship, 23, 35, 45,
103
tests, x, 25, 36, 43, 59
Thompson, Milburn, 71
Tompkins and Bird, 11, 16, 55–56
Tong, Rosemarie, 77
tranquility, 29–30, 48, 63
transformation, vi, viii, xvii, 8, 35, 37,
51, 57, 59, 63, 66–67, 70, 89, 95
Truth and Reconciliation Commission,
19, 69
Tutu, Desmond, 14, 19, 31, 64, 69

unconditional: forgiveness, 1, 17, 23,
64, 68–69, 90; love, x, xi, xiv–xv,
8–9, 13, 17, 25, 28–29, 35–36, 44,
47, 61, 88, 95, 99–100, 102

values, x, xv, 12, 23, 25, 29, 34–35, 37,
45, 49, 52, 56, 66, 73, 78–79, 83,
85–87, 91, 101, 103, 106; central,
25–27; core, 8, 92; and habits, xv,
23, 35, 76, 106; moral, 3; patriarchal,
77
violence, ix, xi; all forms of, 8–10, 17;
global, xiv, 1–2, 4, 7; physical, 18,
26, 28, 33–34, 50, 65–66, 68, 107,
109; wars and, 1–2, 4, 7
virtue(s), xiii–xiv, 4, 31–32, 34, 41–42,
44, 46, 50, 61, 65, 74, 77, 80–81, 86,
88–89, 100
vision, xi, xvi, 2, 9–10, 26, 30, 37, 51,
57, 60, 69–70, 78, 81, 89, 93–94,
95–97, 101, 103, 105

Walsh, Neale, 14, 19, 23
Walsh, Roger, 15, 53, 54, 76
weapons, ix, xi, 3, 18, 24, 33, 59, 90,
99, 103; of mass destruction, ix, xi,
1, 3, 24, 98
well-being, xiii, xiv, 2–3, 11, 16, 24–25,
28, 34, 38, 48, 57, 75, 86, 90, 96–97,
106, 108
wholeness, 6, 52, 56, 64, 70, 72, 81–82,
93
women, 4, 77–81, 101

Yan Xin, 42, 65, 81

yin and yang, xiv, 80, 82

About the Author

Jing Lin is an associate professor of education at the University of Maryland, College Park. She has taught courses in education for global peace, culture and education in a global context, philosophy of education, spirituality and education, gender and education, and society and education in East Asia. She has published on social equalities and education, educational reform, bilingual and cross-cultural education, environmental education, and peace education.

She has done extensive research on Chinese education, culture, and society. She is the author of four books: *The Red Guard's Path to Violence* (1991), *Education in Post-Mao China* (1993), *The Opening of the Chinese Mind* (1994), and *Social Transformation and Private Education in China* (1999).